D0850156

Selected Titles in This Series

The Way I Remember It

HISTORY OF MATHEMATICS
VOLUME 12

The Way I Remember It

Walter Rudin

AMERICAN MATHEMATICAL SOCIETY
LONDON MATHEMATICAL SOCIETY

1991 *Mathematics Subject Classification.* Primary 01A70.

Library of Congress Cataloging-in-Publication Data
Rudin, Walter, 1921–
    The way I remember it / Walter Rudin.
        p. cm. — (History of mathematics, ISSN 0899-2428 ; v. 12)
      ISBN 0-8218-0633-5 (alk. paper)
      1. Rudin, Walter, 1921– . 2. Mathematicians—United States—Biography. I. Title.
II. Series.
QA29.R78A3   1996
510′.92—dc20
                                        96-27190
[B]   CIP

Contents

Preface

Part I of the present book was written in 1992 and was primarily intended for my children. My aim was to record as much of our family history as I knew, and to describe (inadequately, of course) what the world was like in the thirties and forties. I also gave some copies to friends who I thought might be interested in this. Several of them urged me not to stop my tale in 1959, but to write more, especially about my contacts with various areas of mathematics and with other mathematicians. For a long time I didn't think that this was worth doing. But when I was invited to have the book included in the "History of Mathematics" series published by the American Mathematical Society, if I would add a bit more about Mathematics, I accepted.

The added material forms Part II. I tried to describe some samples of my work without being too technical, in accordance with the suggestion that I should write for mathematicians, not just for analysts. I also tried to tell – as well as I could – where the problems came from, what some of their solutions led to, and who else was involved. I hope that I succeeded.

Walter Rudin

Madison, Wisconsin
December 1995

Part I

Prologue

The father of my father's father – Aron Pollak – is the only one of my great-grandparents about whom I know anything significant. He was born in 1817, in a tiny Bohemian village then called Wscheraditz. Its currently used Czech spelling is Všeradice. It lies about 50 miles southwest of Prague.

In 1836, when he was 19, he began to manufacture matches. I don't know where this first factory was located, but in 1837 he already had another one in Vienna, and soon there were several more, scattered across Bohemia, employing over 3,000 workers, plus several hundred old people and children who worked in their homes, in addition to some prison labor.

I remember being told as a child that he invented matches. Nothing I have read confirms this, and I don't know whether he was even directly involved in the engineering aspects of his enterprise. But he definitely was the first to manufacture matches on a large scale and to export them worldwide, packaged in an imaginative variety of attractive match boxes. I saw some of these as a child. His name on them was A. M. Pollak. I don't know what the M. stood for.

He was generous with his money. A newspaper clipping, dated Aug. 18, 1853, from the "Österreichische Kaiserliche Wiener Zeitung" mentions a gift of 40 Gulden, to be given each year to 40 truly needy persons, without regard to religion, on the Emperor's birthday. Another, dated Dec. 24, 1854, is a letter from a priest in Drahlowitz, parish of Wscheraditz, in which he thanks Aron for giving a "significant sum" to a poor Christian father with seven children who had lost everything in a fire. The priest also mentions that Aron had made many earlier gifts, all regardless of religion.

But his largest and most lasting contribution was a completely furnished residence hall in which 75 needy students at the Technical University in Vienna were to live rent-free. He donated 160,000 Gulden for this purpose in 1858 and chose the name Rudolphinum for the building (which was still in operation 80 years later), in honor of Crown Prince Rudolf who was born that same year. Ten years later (Dec. 22, 1868) the building was dedicated, in the presence of Emperor Franz Josef and his son Rudolf, and on March 10, 1869, Aron was elevated to a knighthood.

He was now Aron Ritter Pollak von Rudin.

Now you know where the name Rudin comes from: Aron chose it.

Most of the preceding information comes from the seven-page document that confers the knighthood, bound in red velvet and full of gold lettering. It starts with: We, Franz Josef, by the grace of God, Emperor of Austria, King of Hungary, Bohemia, Dalmatia, Croatia, ..., Archduke of ..., Duke of ..., and the first paragraph ends with etc. etc., etc. Then it explains what a pleasure it is to recognize the merits of "our dear faithful Aron Pollak" and to grant his most humble petition. ("Most submissive" is perhaps a more precise translation of "allerunterthänigst" than "most humble".)

The next page describes his various above-mentioned activities. It is followed by a detailed description of a coat of arms and by an instruction to the authorities that Aron and all his legitimate descendants of either sex should be in perpetuity assured of the undisturbed enjoyment of all the privileges appropriate to their rank. (Exactly 69 years later some of that authoritative tender loving care would have been very welcome.) The document is signed by Franz Josef and his minister of the interior.

To name this student residence after the newborn heir to the throne has until recently struck me as embarrassingly servile favor-seeking flattery. But in light of the historical context and the political events of that period a different interpretation is possible: Aron may have been genuinely grateful for the recent improvement in the status of the Austrian Jews.

Here is a thumbnail sketch of some of the relevant historical background.

In most of Europe, Jews had essentially no civil rights until the end of the 18th century. Depending on when and where, and who happened to be ruling, they were barred from owning any land, they were barred from most professions and many other occupations, they had to wear distinctive hats, they were frequently murdered in large numbers (this was occasionally instigated by the Church, but in many cases no such encouragement was needed) and they were often simply chased out from wherever they lived. For example, in 1492 Isabella of Spain gave "her" 300,000 Jews (who had flourished there until the Inquisition made life miserable) four months to get out or be killed; the wealthy among them had of course to leave it all behind; that same summer she bankrolled Columbus' westward trip to India.

What follows is largely taken from a book which I found on my mother's shelf after her death in 1983. It is a textbook on the history of the Jews, by Kaiserling and Biach, published in 1909, with a statement on the title page that the Austrian Ministry of Religion and Education has approved it for use in any "Mittelschule" (= high school) in which German was the language of instruction. In view of this governmental endorsement it seems likely that the book did not exaggerate the disgraceful facts that are described in it.

In 1670 all Jews were ordered out of Austria. Many went to Berlin, most to Hungary and Bohemia. In 1744 Maria Theresia wanted them all out of Bohemia, and especially out of Prague; the latter was actually enforced. In 1748 they were readmitted, but the number of Jewish families in Bohemia was restricted to 8600, only the oldest son was allowed to marry, and that only after a grandfather had died. Such restrictions varied from one province to another. In Galicia, for example, (the area north of the Carpathian mountains which was then Austrian, later Polish, and is now in the Ukraine) there were no numerical limits, just higher Jew-taxes.

The first Habsburg who showed any benevolence toward the Jews was Joseph II, son of Maria Theresia and brother of Marie Antoinette. The "Toleranzpatent" that he issued in 1782 specified that Jewish students were to be admitted to Gymnasiums and Universities; it opened several professions, did away with double taxes and with special dress requirements. Jews were allowed to own factories and to engage in "Grosshandel" (large-scale trade). But there was no change in the laws that concerned residency and marriage.

Special rules applied to Vienna. To be "tolerated" there one needed government permission and had to pay "tolerance money" (10,000 Gulden in 1786). To add injury to injury, this "tolerance" did not pass from a man to his widow and children (at least not until 1837).

After Josef's death in 1790 things began to go downhill again. In particular, it became more and more difficult to be "tolerated" in Vienna.

1848 was a year of revolutions, when liberals (or socialists or democrats or whatever) rose up against the repressive governments that had ruled most of Europe since the defeat of Napoleon. Every one of these revolts failed, but after the failure of the Austrian one the Emperor was

talked into abdicating because he had made some concessions to the
revolutionaries. And so Franz Josef became Emperor in 1848, at the age
of 18 (and he kept that rank for 68 years, beating Victoria's record by
5 years).

In 1849, religious equality was established: The Viennese Jewish
"Kultusgemeinde" (religious community) was officially recognized in a
public speech by Franz Josef, synagogues and public religious services
were allowed, and special taxes were stopped. But it was only in 1867
that Austrian Jews were finally granted full citizenship rights, with no
legal restrictions of any sort. (The French National Assembly had done
the same thing in 1791.)

Enough of that. Let's get back to the family.

Aron married Betti Goldmann. I don't know when he (they?) moved
to Vienna, but in 1845 their son Alfred was born there. They may have
had other children, but I know of none.

After Aron died "unexpectedly" in the early 1870's (according to an
article written in 1931 after Alfred's death) Alfred continued the match
business until the 1890's when (according to a June 1, 1935, article in
"Der Raucher", a biweekly publication for smokers) it was "no longer
possible to stop the victorious march of the Swedish matches which were
displacing the Austrian ones from the world markets". It is not clear to
me why the Swedes were so much more efficient; the writer of this article
seemed to regard it as so self-evident that no explanation was needed.

Alfred then bought a factory in Pfaffstätten, a small town about 20
km SSW of Vienna, near Baden, where printing inks and other paint
products were manufactured. He was one of the first to drive a car
in Vienna, in 1899, and he constructed a private phone between some
country houses in 1883. (Neues Wiener Journal, March 26, 1931.) He
continued to contribute money to the Rudolphinum, as well as to a
kindergarten which his father had started.

Alfred's wife was Sara Lise Levi. This is her name as it appears on
my parents' marriage certificate, but she was always called Louise, as
far as I know. She was the daughter of Solomon Levi, a physician in
Trieste (then Austrian, now in Italy), and his wife Julia.

Alfred and Louise had three children, first Betti, then Artur 2 or 3
years later, and Robert – my father – 14 years after Artur, on Jan. 7,
1891. He was actually named Adolf Robert, but he never used Adolf –
and it wasn't because of Hitler, at least not yet.

Papa – as he will be called from now on – was an inventor. According
to a curriculum vitae written in the summer of 1940 he started at an

extremely early age. In 1907, less than 4 years after the first flight by
the Wright brothers, he constructed model airplanes with "automatic
steering and stabilizing devices" – something like an autopilot. At the
same time he developed a system for putting a sound track on movie
film, side by side with the picture, but the then existing microphones
and the nonexistence of amplifiers made this a practical impossibility.
He kept returning to this theme over the next 30 years, with much more
success.

In 1914 he finished his thesis and got a Ph.D. in Engineering from
the Technical University in Vienna. The thesis was essentially a problem
of instrumentation, and this became his real forte in later life. The problem was to measure the distribution of pressures and velocities inside a
turbine. Here is one detail that he often mentioned: In order not to have
to record a lot of readings by hand, he placed the dials of several instruments close together so that he could photograph them simultaneously.
Not only did this make it easier to get data, but the data obtained this
way were much more precise and meaningful.

The thesis is dated June 10, 1914, less than 3 weeks before the
assassination in Sarajevo caused (to borrow one of Vonnegut's phrases)
the excrement to hit the air conditioner.

During World War I Papa became an Oberleutnant. At the beginning he was in the artillery, on the Russian front, but he was soon
transferred to an "Elektro-Bataillon" on the Italian front. His principal
contribution there was the development of a device for shooting long
wires or cables; these would then carry high voltage current and were
apparently very effective as obstacles in this very static mountain war.
He was wounded twice and spent the last few months of the war editing a
350 page book, "Die Elektrotechnik im Kriege" which contains detailed
accounts of the achievements and adventures of the "Elektro-Truppen".
The preface is dated Nov. 1918, the month after the collapse and total
disintegration of the Austrian empire. His name appears as Oblt. i. d.
Res. Ing. Dr. techn. Robert Pollak Ritter v. Rudin.

This may be the last time that he used "Ritter". After the end of
the monarchy, such titles were abolished (even though some continued
to use them), and the family name became Pollak-Rudin.

It's time to tell about my mother's family, the Adlersbergs.

Their roots lie in three cities, all under Austrian rule until WWI
and all in the Ukraine since the end of WWII.

(1) Czernowitz, the capital of the region called Bukovina, was called Cernauti while it was in Romania between WWI and WWII. On current maps it is Chernovtsy.

(2) Lvov, also called Lemberg and Livow, was in Poland between WWI and WWII, as was

(3) Stanislau, or Stanislawow, located in Galicia about halfway between (1) and (2). In my 1986 N.Y. Times atlas it is called Ivano-Frankovsk (with Stanislau microscopically small underneath).

Felix Adlersberg, son of Leo Adlersberg and Salamanca Littmann, was born in Stanislau on May 4, 1864, the youngest of several brothers.

His wife, Charlotte Aszkenasy, daughter of Markus Wolf Aszkenasy, was born in Lvov on Oct. 15, 1870.

They were married on Aug. 23, 1891, and their daughter Natalie (she was never called that, she was Natasza all her life) – my mother – was born on June 22, 1892, in Stanislau.

On her birth certificate, Felix is stated to live in Stanislau, Charlotte's parents in Czernowitz. Some time between then and 1914 (probably in the early part of that period) he and his brother Michael acquired about 10 square miles of hilly forest in the Bukovina. The place was called Hilcze (later Helgea by the Romanians), about 20 miles SW of Czernowitz, in the Prefecture of Storojinet (or Storozhinets), near a small town called Banila (or Banilov) on the Siret river. There was a saw mill in Hilcze, and a railroad spur to take the lumber away. I don't know whether Felix and Michael installed that saw mill or whether it existed before they got that land.

I spent two summers there as a child and will say more about it later.

Michael's wife was always called Tante Natalka (she was probably Natalie too). I have a vague recollection of having seen Michael when I was a child, and I definitely remember visiting Natalka in Czernowitz. They had one son, Gustav (or Gustinko); more about him later. I have a feeling that Charlotte and Natalka may have been sisters. They looked alike.

A brother of Felix and Michael, Sigmund (or Zygmund?) owned another piece of land near Hilcze, and there was another Adlersberg in that part of the world, Zygfryd, of my mother's generation, whose exact relation to any of the previously mentioned people I don't know – and perhaps never knew. He too will be mentioned again.

Some time between 1892 and 1914 Felix and Charlotte bought a large apartment in Vienna. She lived there most of the time, he spent most of his time in Hilcze, but they visited each other quite frequently.

I don't know anything about my mother's childhood. When she was 15 she was sent for a couple of years to some sort of girls' finishing school in Dresden which she always claimed to have hated (the school, not Dresden). During WWI she did some volunteer nursing of wounded, but her parents would only allow her to do this in an officers' hospital.

Felix probably spent most of the war in Vienna. Hilcze was right in the middle of some heavy fighting in 1914, and there was a lot of destruction. They obviously had very little income during those years. Probably to make up for this, Felix and Michael sold oil drilling rights on their land, for a period of 30 years, for a down-payment of 50,000 Kronen, plus 14% of any future revenues. This was done in 1919. As it turned out, no drilling was ever attempted in Hilcze.

I don't know how or when my parents met. Two days before they were married, Felix executed a very formal document in which he pledged to give Robert (his future son-in-law) 50,000 Kronen per year. What I find almost unbelievable about this is the statement that Felix was doing this "in fulfillment of his obligation under paragraph 1219 of the civil law...". Did such dowry laws really exist?

The marriage took place on July 1, 1920, and they spent their honeymoon on the Lido near Venice.

CHAPTER 1

Earliest Memories

I was born in Vienna, on May 2, 1921.

At the age of about one year, when I was learning to walk, I grabbed a tablecloth and poured a pot of scalding hot coffee on my left shoulder. Of course I don't remember this, but I still have the scar. The best that medical science could do for me at that time, I was told later, was to remove all bandages and expose the burn to the healing rays of the sun. It worked.

Some time, probably before I was two, I made my one and only contribution to the German language. Grandparents were often called Opapa and Omama, or just Opa and Oma. I must have realized that there were two such pairs of people in my life (and perhaps even that their relation to me was not quite the same) and must have felt that they should therefore be named differently. So Papa's parents stayed Opapa and Omama, but I invented Apapa and Amama for Mama's.

The use of well-chosen terminology was apparently important to me even then!

Many years later my children called their paternal grandmother Amama, which pleased her mightily. At present, the title is vacant.

Vera, my one and only sibling, was born on May 31, 1925.

My first real visual memory is of swimming around and under a boat dock in the Wörthersee, a warm lake close to the border with Yugoslavia (now Slovenia), with some other boys. I was 4 or 5 then. I don't remember ever taking swimming lessons, but I am pretty sure that I did. I wouldn't have been allowed in the water without that. But I do remember seeing others being taught. Here is how that went: You had a big cork belt around your waist, the swimming instructor was at the edge of the pool, carrying a pole from which dangled a rope that was fastened to your belt, and then, like a caught fish, you were to do the breaststroke to the chant of "one – two – three – four" with your head held high out of the water. I still love to swim, especially in the ocean, and I have learned how to dive under a wave when necessary, but the influence of my childhood lessons is still there and makes we feel happier when my face is not under water.

I caught all childhood diseases that were then common, chickenpox, mumps, whooping cough, measles, and scarlet fever. The last three have almost vanished by now, at least in the "developed world" that we inhabit. The measles caused the greatest complications. I was stuck in my room for 6 weeks (even though I only felt sick for about 10 days) with the curtains closed to protect my eyes, the apartment was under quarantine, Mama was the only one who was allowed to have any contact with me, Papa moved out, probably to his parents, and I am sure Vera was taken away too, perhaps to Amama, with Mimi, the Kinderfrau. I don't remember this very precisely. The quarantine business may have happened at the scarlet fever time.

When a child had an ordinary cold with some fever, the patient was fed aspirin and lots of hot liquid (tea or lemonade) and was then tightly wrapped in sheets and thick blankets in order to sweat profusely and to thus get rid of the evil. I well remember the soggy sheets.

One last early memory: I held a peach, very soft and overripe, I didn't want to eat it, and I threw it on the floor. I don't know who it was that reprimanded me for this – it was probably Mimi – but it was quite a scolding, caused by the memory of not having had enough to eat during the war. The message has stayed with me till now: To throw food away is a sin.

CHAPTER 2

The Family

We lived in a large apartment, on Belvederegasse 8, near the Belvedere Park. According to the central European way of counting, we were on the second floor. At street level there was the "Parterre", then came the "Mezzanin", and the real count began after that. So, in American parlance, we lived on the fourth floor.

There was no elevator. We had a large living room, large dining room, a large bedroom for Mama, a small one for Papa, and then a large room for the children which we shared with a "Kinderfrau" as long as we were small enough. Later that room was partitioned by a wall, so we each had our own room. There was also a bathroom, a kitchen, and a maids' room which was shared by a cook and a maid.

Having servants in the house was not regarded as a luxury – it was the middle-class way of life. Having a car, on the other hand, was definitely a luxury, and neither we, nor our grandparents, had one. (Except that Apapa kept one in Hilcze, complete with a driver-mechanic).

Having separate bedrooms was apparently quite common for married couples at that time and place. Sleeping together was considered unhygienic! I remember hearing any number of conversations about the evils of bacteria. An even hotter topic, of course, was psychoanalysis, with the adherents of Freud battling those of Jung. Talking of bedrooms, I once heard one lady explain to another that "a married woman should sleep with her husband at least once a month, for just in case". I don't know how old I was at that time, but I was young enough to be pleased that I understood.

Apapa and Amama's apartment was on Weihburggasse 26, closer to the center of town, just inside the Ringstrasse. It was a very comfortable place, with big leather chairs, and both Vera and I felt very much at home there. Amama had diabetes and gave herself insulin shots every day – something that really impressed me. She had occasional bridge parties and taught me how to play chess.

The relation between Mama and her parents was curious: she never really grew up. When they talked about her, they called her "die Kleine", the little one. Her mother paid for her clothes and other things of that sort. She saw her mother almost every day, and if she didn't, she talked to her on the phone. There was a taxi stand right in front of Amama's apartment, and if Mama was there in the evening she took a taxi (the distance was a mile or at most two) and phoned, as soon as she got home, to announce that she had arrived safely.

Apapa was probably the best looking person in the whole family – tall, very straight-backed, very handsome face.

The relation between Papa and his parents, brother, and sister was polite, cool, and distant. I don't know the reason for this. Opapa and Omama owned a large building diagonally across from the Opera (Kärntnerring 10). The Austrian Automobil Club occupied one floor, their apartment occupied another, and I don't remember what was in the rest of the building. (They had an elevator, as did Amama.) Their apartment almost looked like a museum, filled with big heavy furniture and expensive paintings and Chinese vases and little objets d'art. Children were not supposed to touch.

Vera and I were there maybe two or three times a year, usually on some rather formal occasion. Omama liked Italian food; Risotto was one of the specialties of the house. We spent several New Year's Eves with them. At midnight you were supposed to take a spoon (silver? stainless steel?), put some lead into it, hold it over a candle, and pour the molten lead into cold water. The shape of the resulting blob would then, after proper interpretation, foretell your fortune for the coming year.

Opapa died in March 1931. He was 86 years old, and I remember him as always looking strong and healthy. Omama died later; it is curious that I have no recollection of that event. Vera thinks it was some time in the middle thirties.

At Opapa's funeral I wore long pants for the first time. Boys used to wear shorts in warm weather, and woolen knee socks and "knickerbockers" (baggy pants that buckled below the knee) in winter.

I don't know what Papa's brother Artur did for a living. He probably took care of the factory in Pfaffstätten. He and his wife, Elda, had a son, Dolf, and a daughter whose name I don't remember. Dolf was mainly interested in card tricks. We saw them even less often than we saw Opapa and Omama, in spite of the fact that they lived quite close to us.

Papa's sister Betti married Hugo Fasal, a physician, I think, and had a son, Paul. As I mentioned earlier, she was about 16 years older than Papa, and was either widowed or divorced when I knew her.

Since these people may not be mentioned again, this may be a good place to set down what happened to them later.

Artur's family went to Cuba, probably in 1939. He died there. Elda lived to a ripe old age in Springfield, Mass., where her daughter gave music lessons. Dolf worked as a cutter in some Hollywood studio and also hired himself out as an entertainer at private parties, showing off his magic tricks.

Betti spent most of the war in Shanghai, where she arrived via the Trans-Siberian Railroad. She then came to New York, and I am sorry that I didn't quiz her more about her experiences. She must have had some interesting tales to tell. After a few years in New York she returned to Vienna.

The building on the Kärntnerring – which must have been worth a fortune – was of course "aryanized" by the barbarians. In 1946, Papa received "compensation" for his share of the property. It was just enough to buy a 10 year old Buick – the only car he ever owned.

Let me now tell a bit about Hilcze, the 10 square miles of hilly forest that Apapa owned jointly with his brother Michael. Apapa lived there most of the year although he spent part of each winter in Vienna. I spent two summers there, one when I was quite small and the second in 1936.

As mentioned earlier, Czernowitz was the nearest large town. In good weather one could drive there by car over a dirt road – it involved fording a river. There seemed to be three very distinct classes of people living in that area, the Bukovina: The landowners, who spoke German; the real natives who spoke Ukrainian, or, as it was sometimes called, Ruthenian (the dictionary describes Ruthenian as a dialect of Ukrainian); and the government officials and bureaucrats who spoke Romanian.

Apapa really loved this place. I remember hiking through the forest with him and his forester while they marked the trees that were to be cut. He told me over and over that when you cut a tree you must plant one. There was a nursery for that purpose, and there was no clear-cutting. Getting the logs to the sawmill must have been quite an operation. Horses helped, and according to one document, Hilcze employed between 600 and 800 workers. This sounds like a large number.

Perhaps it includes the families of the workers – Apapa ruled Hilcze like a benevolent feudal lord.

There was a railroad spur that connected the sawmill to the outside world. To assure a reliable supply of railroad cars, which were needed to ship the lumber out, a regular system of payoffs to railroad officials was in place. There were also various inspectors who came around, were properly wined and dined, and left with fat envelopes in their pockets. That was a necessary business expense.

Later, in France, the one thing I remember Apapa to complain about was: "In Romania, when you bribe someone, they do it."

I don't remember what kinds of trees grow in that part of the world, but at least some of the wood taken out of Hilcze must have been quite valuable. In any case, the money that came out of Hilcze kept the family going very well, and was extremely helpful later, during our emigration.

Michael's son Gustl was intended to run Hilcze after Apapa could no longer do it. But he turned out to be an incompetent playboy who flunked out of business school in Vienna. He, and some other Adlersbergs, ended up in Brazil where, according to his uncle, he had to spend a couple of years "in the country". He had apparently been caught in some questionable money-shuffling activities and had not mastered the fine art of Brazilian bribery.

The trip from Vienna to Czernowitz was a long train ride, through Czechoslovakia and across southern Poland, around the Carpathian mountains. In those days all locomotives burned coal, and kids like me who stuck their heads out the window always got some soot in their eyes.

Vera spent another summer in Hilcze, in 1937, while I was on the Isle of Wight in England. More about that later.

CHAPTER 3

Schools

I did not go to any kindergarten.

At the age of 6 I started in the so-called Volksschule. I remember nothing about what went on there during the next 4 years, except that one of the teachers was about as wide as she was tall. I suppose I learned whatever kids of that age are supposed to learn.

At age 10 there were several options. For those who had no academic ambitions (or whose parents had none) there were 4 more years of Volksschule; I am pretty sure that that's what it was called. School was compulsory to age 14.

There were three academically oriented tracks, Gymnasium, Realgymnasium, and Realschule, each lasting 8 years. The main difference lay in the languages taught: Greek and Latin in the Gymnasium, one ancient and one modern language in the Realgymnasium, and English and French in the Realschule. I was sent to the same Realschule to which Papa and Opapa had gone. It was within easy walking distance from our apartment. I had to take an entrance exam, which was no problem.

We had 5 classes every day, from 8 to 1, with a 20 minute recess in the middle of the morning, when we could run around the gravel yard or play some games there. School met 6 days a week. All students and teachers were male. I think that the only females who ever entered the building were mothers on go-to-school nights.

There were about 20 or 25 boys in my class, and we stayed together from one year to the next. We stayed in one room, and the teachers took turns coming in. Many of them had Ph.D's; all were called professor. The curriculum was set. There was no choice, except that electives could be added to what was required. I once added Latin, but didn't pay too much attention to it because it wasn't obligatory and didn't really count.

I will now describe, as well as I can remember, what we learned (or what they were trying to teach us) in the various subjects.

17

Mathematics. Basic algebra and trigonometry came very early. Geometry was quite different from the way it is taught in the U.S. We never heard of axioms, we never proved a theorem. At least, we never heard those words. What we learned were facts, and the facts were established by constructions. Given any three pieces of data about a triangle (angles, sides, altitudes, bisectors, ...) we constructed the (or a) triangle that fitted those data, using ruler and compass. Conic sections were dealt with in this manner, as was some projective geometry.

We spent at least one semester on spherical trigonometry, and a lot of time on what was called Descriptive Geometry. This is more like engineering drawing than mathematics; the game is to represent objects in space by their projections on two planes.

In the last year of Realschule I would have taken some calculus. I didn't stick around for that, but I didn't need to. When I was about 14 I saw a calculus book on my father's shelf and started working my way through it. Pretty soon I knew most of the material that we teach here in the first two semesters of calculus. I also learned enough analytic geometry to find algebraic proofs of the various geometric facts about conic sections that we had seen in school.

German. This, like Mathematics, was taught every semester. Of course we learned grammar and read a lot – the second part of Goethe's "Faust" was a bit over my head – plays, novels, poems – but the most important aspect was that we had to write a lot. Every week or two there was a 4 or 5 page essay to be done, either on an assigned topic or on one that we could choose ourselves. We had the same professor from year to year; his name was Hauke, a nice man. He was our "Klassenvorstand" – class president. I don't know exactly what that implied. I suppose he kept our records, and if any other teacher had some complaint about one of us, he heard about it.

History. This was probably also taught every semester. We spent an enormous amount of time on ancient Greece and Rome, learned details of every battle that Hannibal fought against the Romans, then came the so-called Holy Roman Empire with all its kings, emperors, popes, princes, dukes, etc., etc., etc. Basically, we were taught the history of Mitteleuropa.

English history was ignored. America was probably mentioned without going into details like the Declaration of Independence or the Civil War. The French Revolution and Napoleon were hard to avoid, but the two sieges of Vienna by the Turks were discussed in much more detail.

The Norman Conquest, Garibaldi and the unification of Italy, the Crimean War, those I only heard about later.

The history teacher I remember (I don't think he was the only one we had) was called Gerstenhengst (literally: barley stallion). He once told us about one aspect of the new German criminal code: Convicted murderers were to be beaten with steel whips before being hanged. He thought that was great.

English. This started at age 11 (second year) and continued from then on. The instruction emphasized reading, writing, grammar, but not one of our teachers was a native English speaker. After a few years, I could read everything, could write fairly well, could speak so that people could more or less understand me when I first came to England, but I could hardly understand a word that was said to me.

French. Same as English, but it started three years later.

Physics, Chemistry, Biology. We had a year or two of each of these, but it was all out of books. There was no lab of any sort. In Physics we sat in a steep auditorium and the teacher occasionally performed some experiment on his desk which we could hardly see anyway.

Shop. It was called "Handwerk" and we made little doodads.

Gym. I was bad at it and hated every aspect of it. The only thing I could do at all well was rope climbing. A strange skill to have!

Geography. I enjoyed this, having been a map freak all my life. The teacher, Klapeer, was much more easy-going than the rest of them and told all sorts of stories when he got bored with geography.

And finally:

Religion. Austria was a very clerical country whose government kept in close touch with the Vatican, and religious instruction was part of the compulsory curriculum. The large majority of the population were of course Catholic, the rest were Protestants or Jews. At the time set aside for religious instruction, a priest came to talk or preach or whatever to the Catholics, the Protestants went somewhere else to be taught by I don't know who, and the two Jews went to yet another room which was visited by a rabbi.

Yes, in all the years that our class stayed together, Hans Altmann and I were the only Jews, and he was the only one of my classmates who ever came to my apartment or whom I visited in his. (This was normal behavior for adults as well. Jews and Gentiles did not mix socially.) The

Altmann family later escaped to Czechoslovakia – a safe country, they thought, where they had relatives. They were killed in Theresienstadt.

There was also one half-Jew in our class, Schinka. I don't remember what the other half was, and have no idea what happened to him.

The rabbi actually had students from several grades in the same room, so there weren't just the two of us. We didn't learn much. We went through the Old Testament and learned a bit of Hebrew, just enough to say prayers, we didn't really learn the language.

At the proper age (13) I went through the Bar Mitzvah ceremony. No one in our family was in the least religious, so I don't really know why I was made to go through this. (Memorizing a lot of Hebrew without understanding it was hard work.) Amama and Mama used to fast on Yom Kippur, but I am not sure whether they went to the synagogue even on that occasion. Certainly none of us ever went there at any other time.

Having described what there was in school, let me tell what there was not.

There were no extracurricular activities – no school plays, no bands, no sports, no teams. Kids played soccer, but it had nothing to do with school. There was no cafeteria. There was not even a school library. There was no school nurse, and no psychological counseling.

The only activity of that sort – and it was one that I enjoyed – was an annual week of skiing. The whole class went together, to some hut in the Alps. I also usually went for a week during Christmas and during Easter break. But that was with a privately organized group. After a few years I got to be reasonably good at it.

Apart from Hans, Fritz Kauderer was the only other classmate with whom I had any contact outside school. The common link was that we both liked mathematics. We went skating together but, as mentioned earlier, we never went to each other's apartments.

Of course antisemitism reared its ugly head at school. Usually it was verbal, sometimes physical, but they never ganged up on us (unlike at the University of Vienna, where Jewish students were exposed to much more serious violence). Fist fights were one-on-one. I had a real growth spurt during the summer when I was 14 and that fall, when attacked, I could beat up some of the guys who used to give me a bloody nose or a black eye. One takes one's satisfaction where one can.

As I mentioned earlier, Realschule was an eight year program, but for reasons which will soon become clear I became a drop out (or a kicked-out?) before the end of the seventh year.

CHAPTER 4

Inventions

I find it difficult to write about Papa's scientific work between 1918 and 1938, partly because I was unaware of much of it at the time, but mostly because I know very little about electronics. Much of the information in the next few pages comes from two Curricula Vitae (CV). They are undated, but internal evidence shows that one (in German) was written in late 1938 or early 1939, the other (in French) in the summer or fall of 1940.

In 1919 he became a partner in a machine tool factory. I don't know how long that lasted or why it stopped. On his marriage certificate he is described as a factory owner.

From 1921 on he had his own lab which at first was devoted to electro-chemical research, such as chemical methods for registering the passage of weak electric currents (he patented one of these) and methods for the artificial (and speedy) aging of wine and liqueurs, but he soon returned to his main interest, the electric recording, transmission, and reproduction of sound.

In 1925 he became scientific advisor in a vacuum-tube factory. During that time he constructed and patented a new kind of vacuum-tube which he called Frenotron and which avoided certain types of interference. Production was started, but the factory was forced to close because of financial mismangement. He says in one of the CV's that he had to let the patent lapse because he could not afford to pay the required fees, and that a few years later these tubes were manufactured by others, by the millions, under the name Binode.

In 1927 he was appointed court expert in patent suits involving sound film and radio technology. During the following years he was instrumental in deciding several large cases. He particularly mentions Western Electric and Radio Corporation vs. Siemens-Halske, Tobis, and Klangfilm.

We are now getting into the period within my memory: Papa suggested to me once that patent law might be an interesting field to study.

His lab, on Mayerhofgasse 3, was just a few blocks from my school (Waltergasse). I would occasionally go there after school, we would walk home together, have dinner (the main meal of the day was eaten around 2 p.m.), and then he would go back to the lab and often stay till late in the evening. The lab was a clutter of mysterious gadgets whose purpose and function I understood only vaguely.

In the early thirties he began to produce easy-to-handle recording machines and blank records in his lab, to be used by amateurs for recording radio concerts for later playback (just as people nowadays tape TV programs). He also made records which, for example, reproduced only 3 instruments of a quartet. The idea was that the fourth could use this to practice the missing part. Without sufficient financial backing he could not enlarge the scope of these developments, which also included long-playing records.

His most successful achievement in that direction was the so-called Variacord, an electronic musical instrument with a keyboard like an organ, which produced a large variety of musical sounds, some that imitated existing instruments and some that were rather different. To show what it could do, he rented a concert hall and had professional musicians put it through its paces in a public performance, as a solo instrument, in a jazz band, and as part of a symphony orchestra. It was highly praised by musical critics, but the year was 1937, only a few months before the barbarians took power, so that he had no chance to benefit from this success.

He had lots of other ideas, constructed many kinds of instruments, some for encoding and decoding spoken messages, some for diagnostic purposes (vocal cords and larynx), but he lacked the business skills which would have enabled him to fully develop any of these. I believe that his professionally happiest period came later, 1941-1956, when he worked at Bell Labs and in the Physics Department of Columbia University, where he was highly appreciated.

One other area should be mentioned in which he maintained a lifelong interest: Magic. By this he meant subjects like telepathy, telekinesis, divining rods, and related phenonema. He published two booklets about this in 1921, "Magic as a Natural Science" and "Foundations of Experimental Magic". At the end of the latter he firmly asserts that positive results are the only ones that can prove anything and that negative ones are of no importance. (That's the sort of thing that drives statisticians up the wall.) To justify this principle he suggests the example of a chemist who tries to produce a certain compound, fails repeatedly, but succeeds once, thus proving that the compound does indeed exist.

In 1949, when he came to commencement at Duke University, it gave him real pleasure to talk about these things with Dr. Rhine, head of the Parapsychology Department and fervent missionary in the cause of ESP (extrasensory perception).

CHAPTER 5

Vacations

We never stayed in Vienna over the summer. As soon as school was over (at the end of June, if I remember correctly) Mama and Vera and I would go somewhere for about two months, and Papa would join us for one or two shorter periods.

Two or three times we went to Alt Aussee, a small village in the Alps, near a somewhat larger one called Bad Aussee, on a small and usually very cold lake – in which I went swimming anyway – and lots of hiking trails in the surrounding mountains. We rented a small house there and brought the cook with us, leaving the maid in Vienna. Or maybe it was the other way around.

It was there that I learned to ride a bike, at age 11, on a footpath parallel to a stream. The first time I sat on it, the bike was irresistibly attracted to something in that stream, and without a wobble I rode straight into the water. But I had it under control pretty soon. I was not allowed to have a bike in Vienna, the traffic was considered to be too dangerous. But there were places where one could rent one for a day, and that was o.k. even in Vienna.

Writing about bikes reminds me that Papa had a small motorbike. I remember riding on it behind him. He stopped using it, on the advice of his doctor, after he had a bad fall while skating which gave him a mild concussion.

Once we climbed a mountain from which one could look down on Alt Aussee and I could even spot our house. So I decided to go straight down, ignoring the winding trail. I got home at least an hour before the rest of the party. They were not pleased with me.

Two summers we spent on an Italian beach in a small pension run by a good friend of Mama, Grete Frischauer. This was in Miramare, halfway between Rimini and Riccione on the Adriatic coast. The guests were mostly Viennese. Almost next door was a Viennese-run summer camp which was nice because it furnished company on the beach, and beyond that there was a huge building, it looked like an ocean liner, which was part of another children's camp, this one run by the Italian government – the fascist youth organization, to be precise. They must have had hundreds of kids in there. They marched in straight lines, and all were dressed in identical pink. We called them the flamingos.

On every available wall in Italy there seemed to be political slogans, all praising Il Duce (Mussolini) to the skies.

While there we also visited Venice (very hot, and we had to sleep under mosquito nets), Ravenna, Florence, Pisa, San Marino, and perhaps some other cities. I enjoyed seeing the cities, the buildings, and the various landscapes, but I got tired of being taken to too many museums (I still suffer from that syndrome to some extent) and at one point exclaimed that I didn't want to see even one more broken old Roman chamberpot.

We were in Miramare when the news of Dollfuss' assassination came. People were very worried about what would happen. Read more about that in the next section.

I have already described Hilcze where I spent two summers; the second one was in 1936. Besides wandering around in the forest our main occupation seemed to be eating. The food was fabulous – all sorts of smoked meats, venison, trout which the local boys caught with their bare hands. I tried it too but didn't even come close.

In front of the house stood two tall pines whose branches were so spaced that it was very easy to climb almost to the top, where I liked to sit and look down at the world. This was just after I had taught myself some Calculus and Analytic Geometry, and quite a bit of my time up there was spent going over this and working various problems in my head.

Something else that I often thought about during that summer was how I might escape to Hilcze in case the Nazis came to power in Austria, a distinct possibility even then. As it turned out, I am glad I didn't.

The summer of 1937 I spent on the Isle of Wight, off the south coast of England, near Portsmouth. There was some organization that arranged for 16 or 17 year old Viennese to stay with people in England who wanted to have paying guests. Quite a large group of us met at the station in Vienna, took an overnight train to Ostende, crossed on a ferry, and dispersed in London to our various destinations. The couple to whom I went had two more boys from our group. To some extent this defeated the purpose because we mostly spoke German to each other.

There were about 10 kids from our group in the vicinity – some boys and some girls, which was nice – some Jews and some non-Jews, which all of a sudden made no difference. Viennese apartheid didn't seem to survive the English climate. We soon made friends with English kids with whom to socialize, ride bikes around the island, and hang around in the evenings. Some of this seemed quite exotic to us Central Europeans. I had never seen a "Milk Bar" where one could get things like milkshakes and tomato soup straight out of a can! I took several big cans of sliced pineapple home as a present for my parents, never having seen such a thing in Vienna.

English food had a bad reputation even then, but what we were served by our hosts was fine. My only complaint, I remember, was about the cheese and biscuits (= crackers) that sometimes were the dessert. I wrote home that the biscuits were so dry that dust came out of my ears.

I soon became a well known person at the local post office. Mama spent that summer in Hilcze (Vera was there too) and whenever a few days went by without a letter or postcard from me a telegram would arrive, asking what was wrong, and please write!

At the end of the allotted time our group met again in London where we stayed for about a week, seeing the sights, one of which was my first ever traffic jam: on Regent Street walking was faster than driving.

And then, back to Vienna to start my last year of school there, although I didn't know it at the time.

CHAPTER 6

A Bit of History

In this section I want to describe briefly what happened in Austria politically between the end of WWI and the Anschluss (unification) with Germany in 1938.

In October 1918, after more than 4 years of war, the various pieces of the Austro-Hungarian empire broke away and the empire was no more.

The armistice was signed on Nov. 11. That same day Karl (who had become Emperor in 1916, after the death of Franz Josef) abdicated. The very next day, the Provisional National Assembly declared in Vienna that "Deutschösterreich (German Austria) is part of the German Republic". It is perhaps worth mentioning that a majority of this assembly were Social Democrats. Needless to say, the Allies would not stand for that. The treaties of Versailles and St. Germain (with Germany and Austria, respectively) stated explicitly that no such Anschluss was to take place, and that the name of the country was to be Österreich and not Deutschösterreich.

The treaty of St. Germain was signed on Sep. 10, 1919. But when my parents married, on July 1, 1920, the stamps that had to be affixed to the marriage certificate to make it legal were still overprinted with "Deutschösterreich"!

Politically, the country was divided between "red" socialism and "black" clericalism. Geographically, the division was between "red" Vienna (which had about one quarter of the shrunk country's population) and the "black" hinterland. Two armed semi-military groups formed: the "Schutzbund" (literally: protective union) on the Socialist side, and the "Heimwehr" (home defense), nationalistic, with fascist leanings. The government sided more with the Heimwehr.

By 1932 the Nazis started to win some seats in local (municipal) elections, supported from Germany by people like Göring and Göbbels who came to Austria and spoke at Nazi rallies.

On Jan. 30, 1933, Hitler became Chancellor of Germany. In June 1933, Dollfuss, the Austrian Chancellor who had very close relations with the Vatican, outlawed the Nazi party.

In February 1934, fighting broke out between the Schutzbund and the Heimwehr, a general strike was called, Dollfuss called out the army. They used artillery to attack the "Karl Marx Hof", a large housing project for workers, killing several hundred. I remember hearing the shelling which lasted 2 or 3 days.

Having defeated the Schutzbund, Dollfuss outlawed all political parties, except for the government's "Fatherland Front".

It is somewhat ironic that after all this Dollfuss was assassinated by a group of Nazis on July 25, 1934, during an unsuccessful putsch. (One of the murderers was hanged and later became a celebrated Nazi martyr.) Mussolini immediately sent troops to the Austrian border; the Italians had no desire for a common border with Germany. And Hitler claimed that he had nothing at all to do with all this and promised never to do it again.

The new chancellor, Schuschnigg, was less dependent on the Vatican and looked more like an intellectual than Dollfuss had been. In 1935-36 monarchist sentiments started to grow but never attracted a significant number of people.

Incidentally, Papa was one of these. He claimed that the best thing that could happen would be for the Habsburgs to come back. He may have been right, even though this hope was quite unrealistic.

The Nazis kept agitating. In January 1938 another coup attempt was defeated. On Feb. 12 Schuschnigg met Hitler in Berchtesgaden, naively trying to persuade him to stop interfering in Austria. Instead, Hitler demanded amnesty for all Nazis, and insisted on a number of Nazis to be appointed to high positions in the Austrian government.

On March 9 Schuschnigg made a last desperate move: He announced a plebiscite, to be held on March 13. The question: should Austria remain independent? Large crowds marched around Vienna, shouting "Rot-Weiss-Rot bis in den Tod" (red-white-red was the Austrian flag) and there were even some monarchists in the streets, shouting "Unser Motto, Kaiser Otto".

But Hitler knew all about plebiscites, and he wasn't about to let Schuschnigg get away with this. On March 11, German troops moved into Austria; Schuschnigg ordered that there should be no resistance, to avoid bloodshed, and resigned. On March 12, the occupation was complete, and on March 13 Hitler headed a triumphal parade through Vienna. The Archbishop of Vienna even ordered church bells to be rung.

The previous day's Rot-Weiss-Rot crowd had doubled or tripled or ... in size and enthusiastically switched to "Heil Hitler". And this was not a government-arranged show of welcome. There was no government to organize it. And as soon as the cheering was over, they started beating up on the Jews.

Two footnotes:

(1) This time, Mussolini sent no troops to the border. Hitler sent him a telegram, saying: "Mussolini, I will never forget this." The story is that Mussolini wired back: "Neither will I".

(2) On April 10, a plebiscite was held throughout Germany including the Ostmark (Austria's new name). The question: Are you in favor of the Anschluss? The announced result: 99.75% JA.

CHAPTER 7

Outlaws

Of course we expected the Nazi race laws to come into force, and thus to become the officially designated enemies of the people. What we didn't expect – in spite of the endemic Austrian antisemitism – was the enthusiasm and the vim and vigor with which the self-styled "golden-hearted" Viennese took full advantage of their new freedom. ("Das goldene Wienerherz" was proverbial.)

One of the popular local entertainments during the first couple of weeks was to round up some Jews – preferably elderly, it was more humiliating for them – force them to their knees, hand them a small brush and a bucket of lye (to burn the skin on their hands) and make them scrub political graffiti off the sidewalk, much to the delight of the onlookers.

Jews who owned stores or other businesses had them "aryanized", often by employees who simply declared that it now belonged to them. Some were kind enough to let the owner stay on as an employee.

Jews who owned cars had them taken away, not by any "legal" authority, but by people who just wanted a car. They sometimes came back demanding to be paid for the gas that they had used.

And I did not hear of a single instance where the police interfered, or where a victim went to the police for help. Outlaws don't go to the police.

On the first day of school after the Anschluss several of our teachers and even some students strutted around in their shit-colored storm trooper uniforms. (The Nazi party had been illegal, but had obviously existed.) One of those was the gym teacher whom I had always disliked. He even had a pistol strapped to his belt. A few days later I heard that he had shot himself in the foot. This was one of the very few bits of cheerful news at the time. Another was that Jews were forbidden to use the Hitler salute.

Very soon all Jewish students and teachers were removed from whatever school they were in, some school buildings were emptied of all Aryans (who presumably went some place else), and those buildings were used by the Jews. I don't remember that there was much learning going on there, but I dutifully went.

Personally, I experienced two incidents that are worth describing. One day a woman phoned, wanted to talk to me, and told me to report at a certain time to be part of a cleaning crew at some army barracks. I don't know who she was or how I was picked. Maybe one of my former classmates arranged this honor for me. After some discussion – should I go? should I not go? – it was decided that it was safer to go. So I went, swept some floors and washed some cars. Some German officer didn't like the way I did that and asked whether I had never washed a car before. To which I replied, quite truthfully, that I hadn't. After a few hours they sent me home.

The second incident happened one Sunday morning when Vera and I went to the Prater. This is a large park, perhaps as large as Central Park in New York, between the Danube and the Danube Canal. It was perhaps a foolish thing to do. Suddenly there was a mob, rounding up all the Jews they could find, Vera and I among them, and started to push and shove us in the direction of the Nordbahnhof (a railroad station), shouting "Jews to Dachau" and other such endearments. Some Prussian army officers who happened to be there and had no stomach for that sort of thing broke it up. So we got away with just a scare.

This incident suggests that a couple of things may need further explanation.

First (and this applies also to the sidewalk scrubbing that I described earlier) how did they know who was a Jew? Well, living in Vienna you just knew, just like some can tell a Serb from a Croat, or a Catholic from a Protestant in Belfast. Of course Jews are supposed to have hook noses, but not all do, and some who do aren't Jews. Gestures, body language, are perhaps clues by which members of a particular group can be identified. In 1984 I was on a city bus in Bordeaux, with Ellen, and I saw a man raise his hand at a bus stop. I said: "That's an American." I have no idea how he signalled, but the gesture just wasn't French, it was American. When he got on the bus he came up to me and said: "you're Rudin, aren't you?" I had no idea who he was.

Anyway, it was important at that time and place to be able to tell, and I too had that skill. I lost it long ago because, fortunately, it has been quite unimportant to me for more than half a century.

The second comment concerns Dachau. In 1945 and later, Austrians described themselves as "the first victims of Nazism" and they got away with this fiction as far as world opinion was concerned. The fiction was even supported by the statement that "Austria, the first free country to fall victim to Hitlerite aggression, shall be liberated from German domination" which formed part of a declaration signed in Nov. 1943 in Moscow by the Allied foreign ministers. Sometimes people (and diplomats in particular) sign something that just ain't so. Austria was not a victim at all, but was an enthusiastic participant. Resistance movements became active, sooner or later, in almost every Nazi-occupied country. To some extent this happened even in Germany. But never in Austria. Every Nazi-occupied country had a government-in-exile in London. Where was Austria's?

The real first victims were the German Socialists, Communists, and other prominent anti-Nazis who were imprisoned in Dachau in March 1933, less than two months after Hitler became Chancellor. At that time Dachau was not a place of mass extermination, but just a brutal sadistic forced labor camp where many were killed anyway, even though some prisoners were actually released after a number of years. I met some of these later on in France.

The existence of Dachau, a few miles from Munich, was well known in Vienna by 1934, as were the names of other KZ's that were soon in business (KZ was the familiar acronym for KonZentrationslager), such as Buchenwald near Weimar, Oranienburg near Berlin, and Sachsenhausen near Kassel. Any German who was an adult at the time and who later claimed to have known nothing about this at all was either deaf and blind or suffered from amnesia or was just lying.

Well, back to what was going on in Vienna.

In all fairness, not all Aryans behaved badly, some were helpful.

There was a gentleman, a total stranger, who escorted Mama across the Schwarzenbergplatz (renamed Stalinplatz in 1945) when he saw that she was afraid because of some commotion in the middle of the square.

There was the lady who, in January 1939, took the same train to Switzerland as did Papa and Mama. She had Mama's jewelry in her suitcase, and returned it as soon as they were across the border. Jewish emigrants were obviously not allowed to take any valuables with them.

There was Mr. Gmeiner, Papa's chief assistant in his lab, who went many places and ran many errands that would have been dangerous for Papa. He even went to the barracks where I washed cars and could tell my parents that I seemed to be all right. The lab itself was confiscated, not by a mob, but by the authorities.

Here are some other official actions.

Very soon after the Anschluss, big posters went up all over town advertising an exhibition that showed in graphic detail the terrible things that Jews were supposedly doing to the world, and to Germans in particular. Of course I didn't go to see it, but since it was organized by Julius Streicher, editor of "Der Stürmer", a weekly paper that contained nothing but antisemitic pornography, I could pretty well imagine what there was.

Signs were put on park benches forbidding Jews to sit there.

Papa received a letter saying that since he was of nonaryan origin he could no longer be a court-appointed expert, and ordering him to turn his license in within a week.

Cardinal Innitzer (he who had ordered the church bells to welcome Hitler) was put in "protective custody".

Schuschnigg was brought to Dachau, I don't know when, nor how long he was there. He survived and did some lecturing at St. Louis University, in St. Louis, Missouri, after the war.

Hundreds or thousands were arrested.

Many, to stop them from leaving the country, had their passports confiscated. This happened to Dr. Frischauer (the husband of the lady who ran the pension in Miramare, I think he had been an active Social Democrat) who then committed suicide. His two sons, twins, escaped to England, where I met them again in the Pioneer Corps.

The number of suicides was large enough to prompt Goering to say that he didn't have enough policemen to put one behind every Jew who wanted to do it. The fear of arrest and worse was just too overpowering.

In one respect we were better off than the German Jews. There the screws were tightened gradually, and for the first couple of years there was hope that it would all blow over, that a different government would be formed, that things would get back to normal. As a result, many German Jews procrastinated until it was too late. In Austria it became absolutely clear within a couple of days that the only option was to get out.

I don't know exactly what had to be done to get an exit permit, but our parents very efficiently enrolled us in Swiss schools, Apapa guaranteed to support us financially, so that the Swiss would let us in, and some time in the middle of June, Vera and I got on a plane to Zürich. I am pretty sure that that was the first time anyone in our family had flown. It seemed safer to go through passport and custom inspection at the airport than to have us do it at the border on a train.

I have not been back.

CHAPTER 8

Switzerland

After we landed in Zürich, Vera took a train to Chexbres, a small town east of Lausanne, overlooking Lake Geneva, where she spent the next 10 months in a girls' boarding school, and I took a train in the opposite direction, to St. Gallen, where the "Institut auf dem Rosenberg" – a boys' school – was located. When the conductor saw my ticket he spoke to me, in Swiss German, in vain. I didn't understand a word he was saying. After a while he tried French, and then I understood that the car I was in was going somewhere else and that I should move to another one. It took me a while to get used to Swiss German, but after a few months that problem disappeared.

At the Institute I was enrolled in a special small program which prepared its students for an exam administered by Oxford University and was given in many places all over the world. On passing, one received the so-called Oxford School Certificate, a sort of high school diploma. This was either necessary or sufficient (or perhaps both or neither) to be admitted to a British university. About 40 years later Mama told me that she had had violent arguments with Papa, long before the Anschluss, about where I should go to a university. He was all for the Technical University in Vienna where he had studied, she saw too much antisemitism there and was in favor of England. No one asked me at that time what I wanted to do. (I tacitly assumed that I was headed for the "Technik" and that I would become some sort of Engineer. Mathematics was obviously by far my most favorite subject, but I didn't know that one could be a mathematician, that there even was such a profession.)

After the Anschluss, that question ceased to be a question, and we applied for a visa to England which never arrived, neither in Austria, nor in Switzerland, nor in France. I guess the Home Office didn't realize that I was coming anyway.

The Oxford group lived in a separate house in which there was also a classroom. My favorite person there was a red-bearded New Zealander,

39

Angus Mc Bean (pronounced Mc Bane). He was the "house father", went on hikes and ski trips with us, and taught four of the six courses that constituted our program : Mathematics (trivial stuff, after the Realschule), Physics and Biology (out of books, just as in Vienna) and European History. In that last course I really learned something new. We also took French (about which I remember nothing) and English literature. That year's topic was The Tempest by Shakespeare and poems by Shelley and Keats. The point of that course seemed to be to memorize as much as possible and to learn what sort of questions might be asked and what sort of answers would be expected.

In December I passed the exam. (I knew how to take exams, a skill which all of my children have inherited.)

From among the whole very cosmopolitan student body I remember only one by name, and I believe that he wasn't even in the Oxford program. His name was Schradieck, he came from a city called Providence in a state called Rhode Island (I had never heard of such exotic-sounding places), and when I mentioned Roosevelt – then the only politician in a position of power who was trying to arouse the world against Hitler – his only response was: "My dad says he is a horse's ass." This gave me a new perspective on America.

Sometime during this period I had to go to the German consulate to get my passport renewed. Or maybe I was called in to get a new one. Anyway, from then on it had a big red J on it – guess what that stood for. The existence and subsequent nonexistence of that passport will be mentioned again later.

Between two trimesters I went on a week's trip through Switzerland. I bought a train ticket that allowed me to get on any train at any time. When I saw a nice looking village or town I just got off, checked my small suitcase at the station, wandered around a bit, and then decided whether to stay a while or to get on the next train to somewhere else. It was an easy and pleasant way to see much of the country. One place I stopped was Chexbres, to visit Vera.

Having completed the Oxford program, I took some other courses during the next trimester, including things like typing, shorthand, and English business correspondence. There I learned that a (the?) proper way to end a letter was "I remain, Sir, your obedient servant...". It was hard to believe that anyone would really write like that. But in 1946 I received a letter from the Director of Navy Accounts which ended with "I am, Sir, your obedient servant...".

One aspect of life in Switzerland that was totally new to me was that people seemed to be voting on something or other every few weeks. This was my first look at democracy. Which reminds me that another brief look at history is in order.

The infamous Munich pact was signed on Sep. 30, 1938. Hitler, backed by Mussolini, had browbeat Daladier and Chamberlain to agree to his "last territorial demand" which was the heavily fortified mountain range along the Czech border, the so-called Sudetenland. According to Nazi propaganda, the Germans who lived in that area were so horribly mistreated by the Czechs that they just had to be rescued. The Czechs were not even consulted about this. When they realized that France and Britain would not support them in any way, they thought it was useless to resist, and let the Sudetenland go. Chamberlain brought "peace in our time" back to London in his pocket. Less than six months later Germany annexed Bohemia and Moravia, and Slovakia became a puppet state.

November 10, 1938, was the date of the "Kristallnacht", the night in which spontaneous violence against Jews was organized throughout Germany with their proverbial thoroughness and efficiency.

My parents were still in Vienna at that time. Fortunately they were not physically harmed. They managed to work their way through and over all the bureaucratic obstacles and arrived in Switzerland in January 1939. They had permission to stay in Zug (near Zürich) for not more than 3 months, in transit to Liberia!

This was standard procedure: In order to be allowed into a desirable country, which was difficult, one got a visa for a not so desirable one, which was easy, and used that to get a transit visa to the first one, hoping to get it extended later on. It didn't work. In April Papa received a letter from the Eidgenoessische Fremdenpolizei (Federal Police for Foreigners) rejecting his request for an extension. Somewhat paraphrased, it said:

"We gave you and your wife permission to stay in Zug for at most 3 months because you showed us proof that you would be able to proceed to Liberia without any difficulty. We demand strict adherence to this agreement. If you do not leave at the proper time, your security deposit will be forfeited, and the Police will immediately start proceedings to return you to Germany."

The letter ended with the customary salutation: Mit vorzüglicher Hochachtung, ...

Luckily, we got French visas, for the whole family, about two days before the Swiss deadline. If that hadn't happened, we might all have ended up in Liberia.

Perhaps one shouldn't blame the Swiss for this intransigence. It is a small country that couldn't have handled all the refugees who would have liked to come, and whose neutrality during WWII definitely leaned toward the good side. My time in Switzerland was a luxurious, civilized, almost unreal interlude between what had preceded it and what was soon to follow.

CHAPTER 9

Paris and Paramé

A few years earlier, Papa had met a French engineer, M. Givelet, at an electronics conference. They became friends, and I am sure that it was he who helped us get our visas. He also arranged for Papa to start working on some projects that the War Ministry (the Signal Corps, to be more specific) was interested in.

Papa must have had a labor permit to allow him to do this, but nevertheless we had to show up at the Préfecture de Police at frequent intervals to renew our permis-de-séjour (permission to stay). That usually took all day and was a real pain in the you-know-what. But since Papa was working we began to think that France might become home.

We rented rooms in a hotel on the corner of Avenue Malakoff and Avenue de la Grande Armée. I think it was a fairly cheap hotel. There was a hot plate in one of the rooms where Mama did a bit of cooking, but we usually went to some cheap restaurant for dinner, the sort of place where you got bread and wine "à discrétion" – as much as you want – just as you get ice water in the U.S.

Each week I spent several hours at the Alliance Française, an organization which, among other things, teaches French to foreigners. My French was reasonably adequate, but there was room for improvement. Since there was no sign of my English visa, I began to think of trying to get into the Sorbonne, the University of Paris. I made some inquiries, found out about some Mathematics entrance exam that would be given in the fall, and got a book from which to study.

My memory of all this is strangely nebulous. I must have just gone through the motions, very halfheartedly, realizing subconsciously that these preparations were pointless, that there would be no university for me in the fall.

War was being talked about constantly. Having eliminated Czechoslovakia, Hitler ranted and raved at an even higher pitch about the intolerable oppression suffered by the Germans who lived in the Polish

Corridor. (This was a strip of land awarded to Poland after WWI so as to give her access to the Baltic Sea. It separated East Prussia from the rest of Germany.) Britain and France had a treaty with Poland which obliged them to come to her defense, and they tried to get the Soviet Union to join them in this.

Some time that spring my parents met someone from the Polish Embassy, a commercial attaché. He claimed to be quite unconcerned about all this: The Polish cavalry could deal with both the Germans and the Red Army, no problem. They had briefly captured Kiev in 1920, in the midst of the revolutionary wars in the about-to-be-born Soviet Union, and had apparently lived off that glory ever since.

In the beginning of July Mama, Vera, and I did what we had always done – we went on vacation, leaving Papa in Paris. We went to a pension in Paramé, near St. Malo in the Bretagne. It sounds frivolous to have done this, given the state of the world, but there was nothing for us to do in Paris, our permis de séjour had apparently been sufficiently extended, and being in Paramé was probably no more expensive than being in Paris, perhaps less so. Actually, it turned out to be a very nice summer, until it came to a screeching halt.

Papa joined us for a week or two, in the usual fashion.

There was an English family staying in the same pension, the Chestertons. They were there with their daughters, Audrey, about my age, and Brenda, a few years younger. We became good friends. You will read about them again later.

I spent about two hours every afternoon studying that book that I had gotten. The material was very different from anything I had seen before, quite a bit of (to me) unfamiliar algebra, and not having anyone with whom I could talk about it I think I would have done quite badly on that exam.

All this time the British-French-Soviet negotiations seemed to get nowhere, the Nazi threats against Poland got worse and worse, and one fine day Stalin replaced Litvinov (the Soviet foreign minister) with Molotov, who promptly signed a nonaggression pact with Ribbentrop (the German foreign minister). This is known as the Hitler-Stalin pact.

A week later, Sep. 1, 1939, the German army invaded Poland, claiming that Polish troops had attacked a German radio station. On Sep. 3, Britain and France declared war.

Papa was in Paris at that time, but the rest of us were still in Paramé.

Unlike in 1914, when cheering French soldiers painted "à Berlin" on troop trains and their German counterparts were going to march straight to Paris, I think that no one cheered this time, no one was enthusiastic. From what I have read it seems that not even the German general staff wanted war. This was Hitler's war, and his alone.

Mobilization orders were immediately plastered all over the place, telling various age groups where to report for duty. A few days later, one of these said that an Austrian Legion was about to be formed and that all male former Austrians, aged 18 to 48, were to report to the Stade de Colombes in Paris, bringing a blanket and I forget what else. My enthusiasm was minimal, but I got on a train to Paris, met Papa, and together we went to the stadium to become Austrian Legionaires! We got in just under the wire: I was 18, he was 48.

CHAPTER 10

Internments

As soon as we walked through the gate we realized that there was no such thing as an Austrian Legion. We were prisoners. Austria was part of Germany, therefore we were enemy aliens, and as such we were being interned. Why had they bothered to lie about an Austrian Legion? They could just as well have ordered us to come and be interned. Maybe they thought that the lie would make it easier to get us all there.

I don't know how many thousands of men were in that stadium, but it was crowded. You found a place on one of the concrete benches or on the floor between them, and that's where you tried to sleep. There was nothing to do all day. Some savvy characters had brought pocket chess sets, which relieved some of the boredom. I believe that it didn't rain that week, at least I don't remember getting soaked.

We were fed bread and liver paté, in large cans, the same every day. This diet caused total constipation in me, which was fortunate since the toilet facilities consisted of open buckets which quickly became most uninviting. I was among the lucky ones who were never ordered to wade in there and carry them away to be emptied.

The weirdest thing I saw there was a bunch of transvestites – giggling lipsticked men in dresses and high heels. They were soon taken away.

After a week we were put on a train – in ordinary passenger cars, not shoved into cattle cars like the Germans did to their prisoners – and taken to Meslay-du-Maine, in the Bretagne, SE of Laval. From the station we were marched to an empty field of grass, surrounded by a barbed wire fence. And that's all there was: an empty field. A few days later a large number of tents arrived, each large enough to hold 40 men (and perhaps even more). We got mattress-size sacks which we filled with straw, to sleep on.

M. Givelet, or perhaps Papa's boss, M. Fua, managed after about 3 weeks to pull the appropriate strings to get him released, so that he could continue to work for the War Ministry. Mama and Vera, who had stayed in Paramé because Paris might be bombed, joined him soon and they moved into an apartment on 15, rue Villaret-de-Joyeuse, a small street parallel to the Avenue de la Grande Armée. I stayed in Meslay.

There were about 2,000 men in that camp. (I can't be too sure about that number.) All of us were refugees, German or Austrian. There must have been a lot of "real" German civilians in France on Sep. 3. I have no idea what the French did with them. Probably sent them home. The camp was "guarded" by one officer and a few middle-aged soldiers who conducted occasional roll calls and sold cigarettes at high prices to those who needed them. It would have been easy to get through the barbed wire fence, but no one did it, as far as I know. The problem was: where would one go?

The internees were an interesting mix. Among the older ones, some had been prisoners of war in Russia in WWI. There were some Poles who had kept German or Austrian citizenship in 1918. There were a few (very few) German Jews whose principal complaint about the Nazis was that they hadn't been allowed to join the party, and who were all in favor of a further German advance to the East to save the world from Bolshevism. There were some who had served in the French Foreign Legion and were enemy aliens anyway. One of them had the Médaille Militaire from WWI, France's highest military honor.

There were some Saarlanders who had opted for France rather than Germany in the 1935 plebiscite. Among them was Konrad Heiden, anti-Nazi author of a "History of National Socialism".

(The Versailles Treaty had stipulated that the Saarland, a coal mining region, should be administered by the League of Nations until 1935, when a plebiscite was to decide whether it would become part of Germany or of France. The Nazis managed to announce a vote of 90% for Germany. Many of those on the losing side found it prudent to leave.)

Some people gave lectures in the evening. I played a lot of chess, read many books, and even helped some guy with his trigonometry. He was about to invent radar. (Neither he nor I knew that it had been done.) The fact that he needed my help shows that he hadn't progressed very far.

We were divided into "sections" of about 20. The main reason for this seemed to be the delivery of mail (which worked remarkably well) and of meals. Each section sent one or two men to the kitchen to bring the food. In our section the food was dished out in alphabetical order, someone carefully noted the name of the first guy who did not get seconds, and at the next meal he was the first to be served. Food was

OK and sufficient, though not overly plentiful, as shown by the just described procedure. This being France, we also got wine or the alcoholic cider that is popular in the Bretagne.

Working in the kitchen was a desirable assignment. The cooks were the aristocrats of the camp. Once, when a man asked a cook for a bit of fat, he was told: "You want fat – grab your ass."

Apparently we were not given dishes out of which to eat. I am a bit hazy on that, but I remember a large tin can that had once held paté, which was my bowl. I used a piece of bread at the end of each meal to wipe the last bits of food out of the can. There must have been running water somewhere, but there were only 2 or 3 primitive showers in the whole camp. (The showers were near the kitchen. You took hot water to a bucket about 8 ft. up, then stood under it and pulled something to make the water come down on you.) The toilet facilities consisted of ditches. When there was enough in one, it was covered with dirt obtained by digging another one.

Why there were no horrible epidemics I don't know, especially since the whole field turned into an ankle-deep sea of mud when it started to rain.

In the beginning of December we moved to a nearby place where we had wooden barracks instead of tents and where conditions became a little more sanitary. Otherwise, life stayed pretty much the same.

With so many people crammed together in a small space one might have expected all sorts of quarrels and bickerings and even fights. There was almost none of that. Occasionally one heard things like: "Hey, this is my nail." "No, my coat always hangs here." Real kindergarten stuff, but understandable when there are only a few nails around.

Each section was headed by a "chef de section" who arranged for the various housekeeping chores that had to be done. At 18, I was the youngest in our section (there were very few of that age in the whole camp), and it was tempting to make the kid do more than some of the older ones. But I learned, by speaking up, that I didn't have to be at the bottom of the pecking order. A valuable growing-up experience.

Of course we always wanted to know how the war was going. We had no radios, but got newspapers. Quite often there were large blank spaces in them where the censor had deleted something. After the quick collapse of Poland, nothing much seemed to happen. There was a short Soviet-Finland war, in which the Finns did remarkably well, but that didn't really interest us too much.

What we were interested in was how to get out – not by climbing over the fence, but legally. We were not mistreated, but we became more and more resentful. At the outbreak of war it seemed excusable that the authorities didn't want to look for fine distinctions and simply interned all residents with German passports. But sooner or later they could have found out who was on which side. A small number, like Papa, who had willing friends in the right places, were released. But there was no one in the French government, as far as I know, who questioned the general policy of keeping all anti-Nazi refugees in internment camps.

One way to get out was offered early and often and quite insistently: "Join the Foreign Legion". I had heard lots about the Legion, most of it bad, and had seen former Legionnaires among my fellow internees. So that did not appeal to me in the least. I believe that only very few, if any, took that option in our camp.

Later we were told that we could join the regular French army. That turned out to be more popular. I was one of those who signed up. On March 12, 1940, after exactly 6 months of internment, I was released from the camp and instructed to go home to my parents and to wait there until I got called up.

So I took a train to Paris and moved into the apartment with Papa, Mama, and Vera. One of the first questions Mama asked me, anxiously, was whether any homosexuals had bothered me. Maybe I was ignorant, naive, and unobservant, but (except for the characters in the Stade de Colombes whom I described earlier) I had never noticed any activity of that sort.

Since I had no idea when I would be called I didn't start doing anything interesting or worthwhile. I just hung around and waited.

On April 9, a sudden German invasion of Denmark and Norway put these countries under Hitler's "protection".

On April 17, Apapa and Amama arrived in Paris. There is a strange blank spot in my memory: I remember their presence very well, but I don't remember their arrival at all, even though that must have been a major family event.

Their passports, which I have, contain some interesting information. By August 1939 the Romanian government was already so impressed by the German example that they stamped EVREU and EVREICA on the passports issued to their Jewish citizens. Their Italian transit visas are dated 9 APR 1940 Anno XVIII, indicating that this was the 18th year in the reign of Mussolini (shades of the Pharaohs!). Since their French visas – issued April 8, good for one month in France – are for a visit to

Paramé, they had probably applied for them in the early fall, or perhaps even in August, before war broke out.

On May 10 Germany launched another sudden attack on a pair of neutral countries, Holland and Belgium. In addition to the usual military moves they dropped large numbers of parachutists far behind the front lines, some in civilian clothes, causing panic and confusion. At the same time a large force drove through the Ardennes and entered France on May 12, breaking through in an area that was weakly defended because tanks were not expected to come over that difficult terrain. This enabled them to get behind the French armies – the beginning of the end, so to speak.

Posters went up again all over Paris. This time there was no foolishness about an Austrian Legion. I forget the exact wording, but what it meant was that I was to be interned again. (Papa had aged to 49, and it was our understanding that this did not apply to him anymore.) On May 14, since the army hadn't called me yet, I took my old blanket and a bit of food and presented myself at the designated place, the Stade Buffalo.

I had seriously considered ignoring the posters. It seemed stupid to voluntarily become a prisoner again. But it turned out that going in was by far the best choice, as luck would have it.

After the customary 5 or 6 days in the stadium (it was déjà vu all over again), we were put on a train which went somewhere south of Paris, to a place called Ruchard (I think) which is on none of my maps. We got off the train in the middle of the night. The Germans among us kept complaining on the way to the camp that the Austrians didn't even know how to march in step, we just walked. We were all a bit upset, I guess.

This camp seemed more heavily guarded than Meslay had been.

On May 26 began the "miracle of Dunkirk", the successful evacuation of a large part of the British Army. That same day a smaller miracle happened to me: I was called to the office of the camp commander, given my call-up papers, and told to get out of there and get on a train to Pontivy, in the center of the Bretagne. I am still amazed that whoever it was that sent my papers knew how to get them to me.

I had to change trains a couple of times and arrived in Pontivy the next day. It turned out that what I was joining wasn't exactly the French Army. It was a labor corps, under Army control, composed entirely of foreigners – German, Austrian, and Spanish refugees in my unit of about 100 men. The "Livret Individuel" that I received, as ID, has "Etranger Prestataire" printed on its front cover. Inside it says that I was a "Bénéficiaire du Droit d'Asile" of Austrain nationality. It also says that I was 1m 95cm tall, which added about 5 inches to my height.

We were given uniforms and were put to work moving furniture to prepare housing for refugees from northern France. In the evenings we were free to wander around Pontivy. It was definitely a step up from being interned.

Of course I wrote my parents to let them know my status, and I heard that Papa had been interned after all. On May 22 the police came to their apartment while he was at work, telling Mama that he had to report to the Stade Buffalo that same evening. M. Fua could not pull any strings in this short time, so Papa went in. After the customary period in the stadium he was shipped off to a camp in Audierne, at the tip of the Bretagne, West of Quimper. He must have arrived there at about the same time as I got to Pontivy.

After about a week it became clear that the war was going terribly. The French Army couldn't cope with the German tanks and planes. The Germans had simply gone around the "impregnable" Maginot line that had made the French feel so safe.

On June 10 Italy declared war (Mussolini evidently wanted to be in on the kill), on June 14 the Germans marched into Paris which was not even defended, and on June 16 a newly formed government, headed by Pétain – the 84 year old "hero of Verdun" – asked for an armistice.

German columns were reported heading toward Rennes and Nantes, thus cutting the Bretagne peninsula off from the rest of France. We had no desire at all to be captured in this mouse trap, and tried to persuade our lieutenant to help us get to the south of France. He either couldn't or wouldn't understand what we were so worried about. After much to do he agreed to write individual passes (laissez-passers) for us to get us through French military checkpoints and the like. He later claimed that he had done this, but would only give them to us if the Germans were really close, till then we had to stay together.

On June 18 we heard that German troops were about 5 miles away. That was close enough for our lieutenant. He told us to change into our civilian clothes, but still kept all our passes (if indeed they existed) in his pocket, insisting that we had to stay together, and we slowly started walking out of town. He obviously had no idea of what we were going to do, said something about hiding in the woods during the day and marching at night, which made no sense to me and to another 19 year old with whom I had become friendly, Henry Silberstein. We started to walk faster, and soon lost the rest of the group. We never saw any of them again.

It was the middle of the afternoon, and the beginning of an interesting week.

CHAPTER 11

Escape*

Henry was originally from Berlin, had lived in France for 5 or 6 years, and spoke what sounded to me like perfect French, much better than mine. So we decided that he would do most of the talking to strangers.

During the preceding few days all of us had of course talked about what to do if and when we had a chance to leave. One possibility was to go straight west, to Brest, a large port where one could presumably find transportation to England. The trouble with that was that if we could not get on a ship we would be much deeper in the mouse trap than before and would have to retrace our steps in order to get out of the Bretagne.

Another possibility was to head south-east, toward Nantes, and try to cross the Loire there. We had no idea where the armistice line would be drawn, but the Loire looked like a reasonable choice. (That guess turned out to be wrong. We didn't know of the German Army's passion for Atlantic ports.)

As a compromise, Henry and I decided to go straight south, to Vannes, a small port about 80 km from Pontivy, from which we might be able to go to England, and from where we could also turn east toward Nantes.

We tried to hitchhike, got a few short rides, walked a lot, heard a lot of rumors that the Germans were here, there, and everywhere, and finally, well after dark, got a ride that was going all the way to Vannes. It sounded too good to be true. It was.

The car was stopped by some French soldiers who demanded to see everybody's papers, didn't like ours, and took us to Grandchamp, a nearby village, where their captain interrogated us. Being an Austrian and a German with French military ID's, in civilian clothes, made us a bit suspect, but after we explained, he was about to let us go, when

---

*The map on page 127 shows the places that are mentioned in this chapter.

55

a couple of eager-beaver gendarmes arrived who had somehow heard of our presence and wanted to prove their patriotism and devotion to duty.

They took us to separate rooms at the police station and started to interrogate us again. The first accusation was that we were spies. Or perhaps we were even parachutists? And when we insisted that we were prestataires who had just come from Pontivy, they accused us of being deserters. This was perhaps technically correct, but was a bit absurd by that time, since most of the French Army had resigned, thrown their weapons away, and were walking home.

About 2 a.m. we talked them into phoning Pontivy to verify that we really were prestataires and that we had been allowed to leave. They were told that someone would call back in the morning. So they locked us in a cell and, being exhausted, we fell asleep almost instantly.

Amazingly, they woke us at 7 a.m., with "you're OK, you can go, but hurry, the Germans are quite near". We asked them for passes, to avoid getting arrested all over again. "We can't do that, go to the military command." There we were told: "We don't issue passes, that's the job of the civil authorities." So we walked out of Grandchamp, were stopped by yet another patrol, but when we told them that we had just spent the night in their jail, they accepted this as proof of our trustworthiness and let us go. After some breakfast we got a ride into Vannes, which turned out to be almost more unpleasant than Grandchamp had been.

Hearing that the last boat to England had left the day before, we went to several Army offices, trying to get a little help with transportation or at least some papers that would be more acceptable than what we had. The help we got was zero. When we told one officer that the Germans might shoot us as traitors because we had joined the French army (that fear was our reason for not being in uniform) he said: "So why did you join? You would have been better off staying in internment. There is a camp nearby, for stateless people, we could take you there." We got out fast.

Another one said, with a grin: "Sure, we can give you false papers, with any name you want, just sign up for 5 years in the Foreign Legion" and assured us of transportation to North Africa and started telling us of the fine life we would have there. Just then someone rushed in: "The Germans are coming!" So he dismissed us with "Débrouillez-vous!"

(The best translation I can come up with of this very common advice is a rather lame "look out for yourselves", but this does not convey its real flavor.)

(Later we found out what a phrase such as "the Germans are coming" meant at that time: either nothing, or 3 or 4 guys on motor bikes or in an armored car. Such a show of force was quite enough to make a garrison of several hundred surrender, especially when the possible arrival of dive bombers was mentioned. They did not waste much manpower on this mopping-up operation. After all, the rest of the world was still to be conquered - und morgen die ganze Welt!)

We went back to the port, again found no boat, tried one more military office, were told again "we can do nothing for you, débrouillez-vous" and then decided to head east, in spite of rumors that it was forbidden to leave town, all roads are guarded, and so on.

Vannes was like a madhouse, with crowds milling around and spreading rumors, but the road (on which no one stopped us) was even crazier. It was jammed with cars, trucks, walkers, horses, going in both directions. People from Vannes were evacuating to Nantes, and people from Nantes were fleeing to Vannes.

We got a few short rides and heard reports, which seemed more believable, that German tanks had entered Nantes and St. Nazaire (at the mouth of the Loire), so we decided to try to cross the river between those two cities. We left the car at an appropriate spot, at a small country road going south. It seemed unwise to risk capture by the Germans, carrying German passports with red J's in our pockets, so we tore them up and threw them in a ditch (we really should have done that a day earlier), together with all other papers we had, except for our French military ID which we thought was necessary (though sometimes not sufficient) to pacify French patrols.

We had walked a short time and were almost at the river when a gendarme stopped us but gave us no trouble. A few minutes later we were stopped again, this time by an irate old civilian who had taken it upon himself to investigate all strangers who came to his village (possibly Cordemais). He had fought at Verdun, he was a true Frenchman, he was not going to let suspicious characters like us off scot-free, and so on and on. A crowd gathered who evidently knew well that he was a bit crazy, and we simply walked on. We were almost at the river, and when we saw boats we went to a nearby house and asked about crossing.

Suddenly, all looked well. The lady to whom we spoke said that the tide was too low now, her husband was already asleep (it was close to midnight), but he would wake us at 5 a.m. and take us across. Then she gave us a very nice supper and led us to the barn where we could sleep on the hay.

When we woke up, before 5, the man was ready with his boat. We took off, in the early morning fog, saw the sun rise when we were in the middle of the wide river, and soon reached the other side, feeling enormously grateful to our boatman and his wife for being so helpful to total strangers, in spite of the risk involved.

When we stepped ashore we were in an area of small country roads with very little traffic. Soon it got hot. We stopped at a farm house and asked for a drink of water. We got that, and a big breakfast!

That morning we walked for 5 hours before we got a series of rides, taking us to Bourgneuf, Challans, St. Gilles, La Roche-sur-Yon, and Fontenay-le-Comte. Every one of these towns had been rumored to be in German hands. We did not see a single German, but saw crowds of French soldiers walking south, without arms or any organization. Some of them talked quite freely about how they were led to believe that they were just as strong and well-equipped as their enemy, and how totally unprepared they were for what actually hit them when the Germans suddenly attacked, eight months after the declaration of war. And now their officers had just driven off in cars, leaving them to their own devices.

The only troops we saw on the roads who had kept weapons and discipline were Polish.

Our last ride that day was in a truck that stopped for the night before reaching Niort. We got out and slept in a field.

Next morning (June 21) we continued hitchhiking, toward Cognac. Henry's father had been working in a Paris bank that had a branch in Cognac and he hoped to find news of his parents there and perhaps get some money; we had very little.

At the outskirts of St. Jean d'Angely the car in which we were riding was stopped. No traffic was allowed to enter the town, so the car had to detour around it. While they had us stopped they also wanted to see papers and didn't like ours. If the car had been allowed in, we would have been driven right to the Bureau de la Place (the local military office) but since we apparently didn't look too dangerous we were told to report there and how to get there on foot.

Needless to say, after our experiences in Grandchamp and Vannes we did no such thing but simply walked straight out the other side of town. No one stopped us. We continued to hitchhike to Cognac, arriving in mid-afternoon. At the bank, Henry learned that the last news from his mother was from Paris and that his father was in a camp near Bordeaux, but he cheered up a bit when they let him withdraw 5,000 francs from his parents' account.

Hitchhiking had become more difficult because gasoline was running out, so we tried to buy bikes. At the first few bikeshops they just laughed: It's easier to steal a bike now than to buy one. Finally we located two, in bad shape, but were promised that they would be fixed up by 8 p.m. While we waited we had a meal and a hot bath (no luxury) in a bathhouse. About 10 p.m. we got our bikes, rode out of town, were stopped by a patrol which, for a change, thought we were OK, found a bit of grass under a tree, and fell asleep.

Next morning we hit the main road from Angouléme to Bordeaux, at Barbezieux. Biking was easy and fast on that road, and we thought we would go straight to Bordeaux, try to get to England from there, and, if that didn't work, ride on to St. Jean-de-Luz where my uncle Zygfryd was staying in a pension and where I thought that Mama might have gone with Vera. She must have mentioned this possibility in a letter to Pontivy.

That morning we met large groups of Spaniards. They had fought for the democratically elected Spanish government in the civil war that Franco won, with the help of German and Italian troops, after almost 3 years of bitter fighting. They had then fled to France where – in spite of not being enemies in any sense whatsoever – they had spent a year in an internment camp (the French government evidently wanted to maintain friendly relations with Franco) and had later become prestataires, just like us. They looked totally lost, hoping to be allowed to stay in France, definitely not wanting to return to Fascist Spain.

We were stopped at the border of the Département Gironde (in which Bordeaux is located); no civilians were allowed to enter, because there were too many refugees there and food was running out. Our military papers didn't help, since we were not in uniform. So we were forced to start on a long detour, slowly, over steep roads. That evening we stopped at a farm house, just before reaching St. Foy-La-Grande, and asked whether we could sleep there. They already had several guests, refugees from northern France, invited us to have dinner with them, and then, after sitting around and swapping stories and trying to guess what the armistice terms might be (it was signed that day), came the big surprise: they had beds for all of us!

Next morning (Sunday, June 23) we still had to go east to stay out of the Gironde. On a particularly rough road the spring under my saddle broke. We stopped at a garage, near Bergérac, and got a piece of wire to hold it in place. In the same garage there was an army captain whose bike also needed some repair. Having nothing better to do, he wanted to see our papers. He didn't like them, but being in a hurry to get away, what could he do with us? Just then, four gendarmes came by. He stopped them, ordered them to arrest us, wrote their names down, and rode off. Those four guys were running away themselves and really wanted nothing to do with us, but they were afraid to just let us go. One of them phoned the Bureau de la Place in Bergérac, asked what to do with us, and was told that someone would come immediately to fetch us.

That was at about 9:30 a.m. We sat around, had lunch with them, sat around some more, until one of them phoned again at 3 p.m. He told us then that we should report to the Bureau de la Place, and emphasized that we should really go there because they had our names and were expecting us. So we rode off, debating, should we? should we not?

When we got there we saw a big sign: No more passes. So we decided to go in, ask for passes to St. Jean-de-Luz, and if they kicked us out we could afterwards say, truthfully, that we had been there, as ordered. We told our story to someone who sat behind a desk, he went to a back room, came back a minute later, wrote both our names on a small piece of paper, and stamped it. We finally had our passes – we were "en règle" – and from that moment on we were not challenged even once to show them.

On the way out of Bergérac we had to cross a bridge that was blocked by several cars filled with rocks, but bicycles could squeeze through. The next large river was the Garonne. We hoped to cross it that evening, but it started to rain, so we stopped at a farm house, just short of Marmande, where they let us sleep in the barn.

Next morning, Monday, it was still raining. We rode into Marmande and looked for raincoats. Of course there were none to be bought. We mentioned to the lady who ran one of the stores that we were heading toward Bayonne, whereupon she said that her son was about to drive there in his truck. Being an Air Force pilot he had been able to get gasoline. When he came by he agreed to add the two of us to his passengers, and we covered those 200 km – two days of biking – in a few hours. A totally incredible piece of luck!

Nothing was leaving for England from the port of Bayonne. We decided to ignore a ship bound for Morocco. Then someone told us that there were several in the harbor of St. Jean-de-Luz, about 20 km further south, ready to go to England. So we got on our bikes and rode on.

It was still raining, there was a strong wind blowing into our faces, the road went up and down, and under the circumstances we didn't fully appreciate the beautiful coast line. It took us almost two hours to cover that short distance.

The port was crowded with Polish troops and hundreds of civilians, pushing, shoving, yelling, and stepping on each other's feet. There were small boats taking people to ships that were anchored at some distance, and that were really going to England. A British officer wouldn't let us on one of the boats because we had no passports. A Polish officer wouldn't let us go with his troops because we were not in uniform. But we kept on trying until it was announced that the sea had become too rough for the small boats. We were assured that there was room enough for everyone and that the embarkation would continue next morning.

By that time it was about 10 p.m., and we started looking for the pension where Zygfryd was or had been. I either remembered its name, or perhaps I had kept a piece of paper with addresses. Anyway, we found it, soaked to the skin and looking thoroughly disreputable, but when I explained who I was, the two ladies who ran the pension became very friendly. They told us that Zygfryd and his family had left on June 22, two days ago, to go to Portugal, and that Mama, Vera, and the grandparents had also been there, till June 23, when they left to go to Biarritz. Till that moment I hadn't even known whether Mama and Vera had left Paris or not. So that was good news. We had passed through Biarritz on our way from Bayonne, having no idea that they were there.

The ladies served us dinner, gave us a room for the night, and refused to get paid for any of this. We got up early next morning, told them that we would again try to get on a ship, and mentioned that if that failed we might try to get into Spain. One of them told us how to find one of her cousins who lived in the mountains and who could show us how to cross the border. Our reception in Spain would probably have been very unfriendly. I might not even have tried this, I might have gone back to Biarritz to find my family.

Luckily, this choice did not have to be made. After several more hours of pushing and shoving we did get on one of the embarkation boats. There were five cargo ships at anchor, one Dutch, one Belgian, three British, plus a British destroyer. We were taken to the "Baron Nairn", going to Plymouth. About 1 p.m., one week minus two hours after we walked out of Pontivy, we steamed away from the French coast!

The armistice had come into force early that morning. That same evening the BBC announced that German troops had occupied every port on the Atlantic coast of France, all the way down to the Spanish border.

It was a narrow escape, hindered by too many obstacles put in our way by antagonistic officials, but made possible by amazing amounts of kindness and help from just ordinary people, by large doses of luck (suppose it hadn't rained that Monday morning in Marmande), and by our determination not to quit at any point but to keep going.

For the first time in my life I felt that I had really accomplished something. It felt good.

CHAPTER 12

Vichy France

I was the only member of my family who got away to England. This chapter will tell what the others did at that time.

Apapa and Amama left Paris by train on May 28 to return to Hilcze the way they had come, through Italy and Yugoslavia. When they reached the Italian border, the Italians had closed it (anticipating a declaration of war?) and the French border guards sent them back to Marseille where they could "surely" find a boat to take them to Romania. They even extended their exit visas for a full two days! Needless to say, there was no such boat, so they stayed in Marseille for about two weeks and then joined Zygfryd in St. Jean-de-Luz.

They were actually lucky to have been prevented from returning to Hilcze because Romania (under considerable pressure) ceded the Bukovina to the Soviet Union at the end of June. Hilcze was of course confiscated or nationalized or collectivized or whatever you call it, and since the Soviet government was not particularly fond of land owners it is not at all clear what would have happened to them personally if they had been there.

Mama and Vera packed most of the family's belongings into a couple of large suitcases which they shipped to Zygfryd. They got on a train, sometime in the first half of June, with only some light hand luggage, and arrived in St. Jean-de-Luz a few days later. Train traffic was pretty chaotic at that time.

The four of them went to Biarritz and then managed to get a taxi to take them to Pau. I imagine that there were two reasons for choosing Pau. From where they were, it was the nearest city in the unoccupied zone, and they had earlier discussed the possibility of going there with Papa because there were plans to evacuate his boss' factory to Pau. (It was a very small factory!)

Papa's story, as told in a letter written about a year later, is much more eventful. As I mentioned before, he was interned in Audierne, almost the westernmost point of the Bretagne. The "camp" was in an empty factory that was surrounded by a 20 ft. high brick wall. On June 19 (the day after I walked away from Pontivy) the internees became so insistent that they had to get away before the Germans arrived that the captain in charge of the camp promised to remove the guards that evening. Instead he doubled them. So the next day there was a mutiny: Some of the internees climbed on boxes and started to knock bricks from the top of the wall. The guards tried to stop this, but being heavily outnumbered and not wanting to shoot, they couldn't.

Suddenly two German soldiers appeared on the wall. The guards dropped their guns and disappeared into the canteen. Then two more Germans came, one of them a corporal. The captain handed his revolver over. There were some "real" Germans among the internees who now demanded (with the Hitler salute) that the non-aryans be separated from the aryans; this was done. When the non-aryans asked the corporal what would happen to them, he said: "Don't worry, we won't do you any harm, our orders are just to keep you here. Of course that could change when the civil administration takes over." Then they tried to organize the cooks, and while they weren't looking Papa and about 20 others climbed over the wall where it had been lowered a bit and walked away.

They separated to be less conspicuous. Papa threw all his papers, note books, etc., in the ocean and decided to be a réfugié français du nord who had lost his papers.

Walking on the beach he got sand into his shoes which made his feet very sore. Next day, after having spent the night in a forest, his feet were swollen and infected. In the evening he came to a village with no pharmacy (he was looking for iodine), and the doctor whom he found wanted to have absolutely nothing to do with him: "Iodine, that's something that you can perhaps find in Paris, but not here. Don't give me any trouble, get out." Strange behavior for a doctor.

Papa spent another night in the open, then found a refugee center where he stayed three days and let his feet improve. During that time he went to the city hall of the small town where the refugee center was. The mayor was very sympathetic. He gave him an official looking properly stamped paper which said that Robert de Rudin, born in Vienne (there is such a town in the south of France) should be allowed to travel to look for his family in St. Jean-de-Luz and Pau. Papa's French must have been much better than mine to get away with this!

He got on a bus to Quimper and then on a train to Nantes. That city was full of German soldiers, the first he had seen since Audierne. He again spent three days in a refugee center – a place to sleep and get some food. The soldiers had evidently been given strict orders to be on their best behavior. They crowded the stores and paid, in French money, for everything they bought. Papa wandered around, being helpful as an interpreter, just to find out what they were talking about and what was going on.

When he tried to get into the train station, his laissez-passer issued by the kind mayor was no good anymore. He now needed a Passierschein, and the only place to get one was the German Kommandatur. He wasn't worried about army officers, he had already talked to several and had aroused no suspicion, but he didn't know whether the Gestapo had set up shop in the Kommandatur. To find out, he asked an officer in the street where the Gestapo headquarters was. "There is no Gestapo here, there is only us, the army" was the reply.

So he went to the Kommandatur, told a lieutenant at the door that he was a former WWI Austrian officer who had lived in France for many years and needed to travel south to find his family that had been evacuated. The lieutenant told him where to go in the city hall to get the necessary form and to bring it back to be stamped and signed. In the city hall they thought that this was most irregular, that one first had to go through all the usual administrative channels, that he would never get out of the Kommandatur once he was in, etc. But he managed to get a form, took it into the lion's den, emerged a few minutes later with his Passierschein, and got on a train south. He had guts!

Since Bordeaux was still out of bounds, the train only went as far as La Roche, where Papa had to spend another three days. Since his Passierschein also entitled him to use army transport, he inquired about that. One officer told him: "What a pity that you were not in Vienna when we marched in, you should have seen the enthusiastic welcome they gave us there, if you come back tomorrow I'll show you some pictures" and another said "You must meet Lt. so-and-so, he would love to talk to another Viennese" whereupon Papa decided not to come back – he might have been recognized.

However, he saw two contradictory messages being posted on a wall, side by side, at the same time.

"All traffic out of town is strictly forbidden. No one is allowed to leave, by train, by car, by bike, or even on foot. All who try to leave risk being imprisoned. Signed: The Mayor."

"All refugees are urged to return to their permanent homes as soon as possible. The authorities will do all they can to facilitate their journey. Coupons for free train tickets will be available at window 32 at the Prefecture. Gasoline coupons will be issued in office 7. Signed: The Chief of Police."

So he got a train ticket, went to Bordeaux, and on to St. Jean-de-Luz. This must have been around July 3. The conversation at Zygfryd's pension was a bit confused, since he was still a "réfugié français du nord", a distant relative of Mme. P. R., but he found out that we had all been there and that I was probably in England. Moreover, there was a postcard from Mama, asking for her mail to be forwarded to Pau.

Next morning, having spent the night at the pension for free, just like I had, he used his last money to buy a train ticket to Pau. At the border between the occupied and unoccupied zones there was just one German soldier checking papers, and he was so glad to find someone who understood German that he let Papa through.

And so they were all together in Pau.

A few days later they moved to Nice. One reason for the move may have been that a U.S. Consulate was there. Nice was too crowded for them to get a permis-de-séjour, and without that there was a very real risk of being interned once again. (There was a large camp in Gurs, near the Pyrenees, just for that purpose. It also held many female internees.) But they were allowed to stay in Avignon, where they settled into a hotel at 14, Place Crillon, having no idea how long they would be there.

To pass the time, and to further his daughter's neglected education, Papa taught her some mathematics and physics while they were there.

The country was now a full-fledged fascist state, commonly called Vichy France, because that's where the Pétain government had moved when they left Paris. The République Française no longer existed. In its place was the Etat Français. On the soon to be issued new coins, "Liberté, Egalité, Fraternité" were no longer mentioned. The new slogan was "Travail, Famille, Patrie" and on the other side was the double-bladed fascist ax, aping Mussolini's symbolism.

But much worse than any symbolism was the notorious Article 19 of the Armistice Agreement: "Any German national in the unoccupied part of France who is wanted by the German authorities will be handed over to them."

This agreement to surrender on demand was not a mere scrap of paper. On the contrary, the French police were only too happy to oblige their colleagues in the Gestapo when called upon to find someone. Intellectuals were particularly well represented on these lists, just like, for example in Poland where their extermination was a deliberate German objective. (The first post-war issue of Fundamenta Mathematicae, vol. 33, 1945, starts with a long list of Polish mathematicians who were murdered, with details where available, and also mentions some mass deportations of entire university faculties.)

As a reaction to "surrender on demand" members of the American intellectual community drew up lists of people thought to be particularly endangered and tried to get emergency visas for them, cutting through much of the usual red tape. These efforts were quite successful. Much of the credit for this American help belongs to Mrs. Roosevelt who persuaded her husband to give the necessary orders.

My parents were not sufficiently prominent to be on any of these lists. But they, and many others, received a lot of help from a devoted group of American Quakers who came to France for the purpose of helping refugees with their emigration and immigration problems. My parents were thus able to leave France with Vera, in May 1941, a year after the French collapse. They spent a few days in Madrid, then 2 or 3 weeks in Lisbon, waiting for their passage, and arrived in New York in June.

Apapa and Amama were still waiting for their visas and had to stay in Avignon.

CHAPTER 13

De Gaulle's Army

We spent three days at sea after leaving St. Jean-de-Luz. Our boat was of course extremely crowded, with hardly enough room for all to lie down on deck, and there wasn't much food, but none of that mattered. I don't know whether the five boats that we saw in the harbor sailed in convoy, with the destroyer as escort, or whether each went its own way. I was too much of a landlubber in those days to pay attention to such matters.

We met another Austrian prestataire on board, Albert Levi, not from Pontivy, and made friends with a few French officers and soldiers who were responding to de Gaulle's appeal to form a Légion Française in Britain and to continue to fight. This looked like a good group to join. When we got to Plymouth and boats came alongside to take people ashore, the three of us just stepped into the one that was for the Free French, as they were called. On the pier there were two officers, one British and one French. We showed our Livrets Individuels, the British officer asked "Are they all right?", the French officer said "They're all right", and we stepped ashore. It was so simple!

Ashore we (the Free French) were cheered by a large crowd, got tea and sandwiches which we wolfed down after three days of very little food, and were given leaflets with the text of the French armistice. That's when I first read about "surrender on demand".

We were told to go by train to Birkenhead, near Liverpool, which was one of the gathering places for French troops. It didn't matter that we had no British money, no one bothered about tickets. The same happened at a couple of station restaurants when we had to change trains: they simply fed us for free. In Birkenhead, when we had to pass through ticket control, of course we had none, we had no papers authorizing us to use a train, and half of us weren't even in uniform. But when we told the man that we were French soldiers and had just come from Plymouth, he not only let us through but went outside to

69

show us which bus to take. How different from our recent experiences in France! And the bus driver, instead of insisting that we pay, offered us cigarettes.

The French camp was at the edge of town, in tents. Most of the soldiers in it had been in Belgium and Dunkirk, had had quite enough of the war and of fighting, and opted to be repatriated to France. They actually left two days after our arrival, on their way home, via Morocco. There was also quite a large group of Senegalese, pitch black with gleaming white teeth. I don't know what their destination was.

I picked up a discarded uniform. When I walked around town in it, little boys crowded around and wanted souvenirs and autographs. The Free French were certainly popular!

One night I was put on guard duty. I was given a rifle and had to present arms every time an officer went by. I had only the vaguest idea how this is done, but nobody complained.

Henry, Albert, and I began to be concerned about our status. For various reasons we would have preferred to be with a British unit but we didn't know whether that was possible. When we asked whether foreigners (i.e., non-French) could join the Free French, we were told that that was no problem, we could enlist if we wanted to. It all seemed very informal, no one pressured us to do anything, so we didn't.

Four days after our arrival in Birkenhead, those who had chosen to stay (about 200) were sent to London, to Olympia Hall. There we found several hundred young Frenchmen, most of them under 20, who had come across the Channel from the Bretagne in response to de Gaulle's appeal. Everyone got a mattress and two blankets and found a spot somewhere in this large building which, I think, had been an exhibition hall.

Even though we had not enlisted we were supposed to choose in what branch we wanted to serve. Henry picked tanks, Albert and I picked aviation. We had a hard time finding the guy in charge of aviation, he was supposed to be someone in a blue suit with a badge on his left arm. When we found him after several failures he seemed pleased to have such a fine pair of recruits: "What we needed was a better air force." However, when his group left London a few days later, Albert and I were left behind. Someone higher up had apparently decided that foreigners were not wanted in aviation. We were told to join the Foreign Legion (déjà vu!) large parts of which were in England, back from Norway. We ignored that advice.

There was of course a big to-do on July 14, Bastille Day, with parades and speeches and all that.

A couple of days later we were sent to Delville Camp, near Aldershot, a large permanent Army camp, south of London. The three of us were together again, this time in the "artillery". (The quotes are there because in the more than two months that I spent there we never got near anything that looked like a gun. I suppose that the British, having lost enormous amounts of equipment at Dunkirk, had none to spare for training the Free French.) We were in very comfortable barracks, got British uniforms with shoulder patches that said FRANCE, and were paid and fed.

One strange thing about this period is that I have absolutely no recollection of what we did all day. There were movies and shows in the evenings, and one could get an occasional pass to London, but I remember no training of any sort, nor do I remember any work that we had to do.

But I do remember watching the Spitfires and Hurricanes attack the Luftwaffe bombers and their Messerschmidt fighter escorts. This was the beginning of the "Battle of Britain" when the Germans were trying daylight bombing of RAF airstrips and harbors, in preparation for an invasion. Planes were fairly slow then (by present-day standards), about 300 mph, and one could easily watch their manoeuvers. The RAF inflicted such heavy losses that the Germans almost stopped daylight raids after about a month and switched to night raids on London and other large cities.

One got so used to seeing planes overhead that once, when I looked up, it took me a few seconds to realize that what I was seeing was birds!

We were of course concerned about the status of German and Austrian refugees in Britain. Those who lived on the South or East coasts had been ordered to move away in the middle of May, when there were lots of reports of German parachutists in Holland and Belgium receiving help from saboteurs ("fifth columnists") who had been planted there much earlier. Some were also interned. But British internment seemed to be different from French: they were sent to the Isle of Man, in the Irish Sea, and were housed in unused tourist resorts. (Even so, internment was no picnic.) Another, much more important, difference was that whereas in France no one gave a damn, there was strong public opposition to this policy in England. Questions were asked in Parliament, as well as in newspaper editorials: why are we doing this to our friends? I believe that most of them were released fairly soon.

Sometime in August I contacted Mrs. Paula Traub, a former Viennese, who lived in a small house in Wimbledon with her daughter Marie-Louise and another lady. And this brings me to another totally blank spot in my memory: I have absolutely no recollection of having known her in Vienna, or of having talked about her with my parents in Paris, or of knowing anything about her at all, but of course I must have, otherwise how and why would I have looked for her? Anyway, she was a friend of my parents, and it was through her that I got my first news from them, in the middle of September.

Before then, all I knew was that Mama and her parents and Vera had gone to Biarritz and that Papa had been interned in Audierne. Now I knew that they were together again and wrote a letter to "Dear Robert and Natasza". I thought it best not to let the Vichy censor know that they had a son in England.

We had a friend in New York, Bianca Steinhardt, who was somehow related to the Italian side of Papa's family. She was a gynecologist, and one of the very few who was smart enough to leave Vienna and come to the U.S. in 1934 or '35, when it was easy. She took the required exams in New York and had a successful medical practice there. She sponsored my parents' immigration. They must have written her that I was probably in England, and she probably sent their address to various friends in England. That's how the news reached me.

Well, back to the Forces Françaises Libres. They finally decided that we really should not be there, that the Foreign Legion was the proper place for us. At that point, Henry, Albert and I split up. We all ended up in the Pioneer Corps, but we did it separately. Never having enlisted, we were free to leave. Not only that, they even gave me a Certificat de Cessation de Paiement! It was like getting a divorce without ever having been married.

So I bid them a fond adieu and went to a British Army recruiting office in London. That was on Sep. 27, 1940. Much later, in 1944, I again spent a few months with the Free French, under much more positive circumstances.

CHAPTER 14

Pioneer Corps

At the Recruiting Office I received a card certifying that I had applied for enlistment, which I took to the Wimbledon police station where they registered me and gave me a ration card. Mrs. Traub had invited me to stay with them until I was called up. I was of course happy to accept. This was the beginning of the Blitz, the nightly air raids on London. The three ladies spent most of their nights in their small basement but I just stayed in bed. It was too crowded down there, and Wimbledon didn't seem to be one of the target areas.

During the days I mostly just wandered all over London. The Blitz has been described so often, by much better writers than I am, that I won't say anything about it, except that it was fantastically impressive to see how people tried to lead as normal a life as possible. Their confidence was amazing. The more they were bombed the more determined they seemed to be not to give in. Losing a war just wasn't done.

I had to wait almost six weeks for my medical exam, and six weeks is a long time to have a house guest. Relations became a little strained at times. The fact that the Traubs had U.S. visas and were nervously waiting for transportation may have been a contributing factor. Having nowhere else to go, I stayed on, even after Marie-Louise's birthday party (she was in her twenties) to which I was pointedly uninvited; I was told not to come back to the house before a certain hour.

To make things even worse, I failed the medical exam. They claimed that I was underweight (140 lbs.) for my height (6 ft.). However, I persuaded the Captain in charge to let me try once more, and two weeks later I passed. I don't know whether I had gained weight or whether the Captain had passed the word to the examiner, or what the reason was. Anyway, on Nov. 20, 1940, I became a soldier in the Pioneer Corps of the British Army.

The P.C. was then the only part of the army that was open to foreigners. I spent 3 years and 2 months in it, almost all of it in or near

73

Catterick Camp in Yorkshire. Rather than give a chronological account of that period, I will describe various aspects of what life was like.

The P.C.'s primary purpose was work. But unlike the Prestataires it was a regular part of the army, having just a few companies that were composed of foreigners. My "Soldier's Service and Pay Book" – the ID that one always had to carry – made no mention of nationality, and we had exactly the same pay, same uniforms, same leaves (one week every three months) as the British soldiers.

Each of us had his own rifle. "Your rifle is your best friend" our instructors told us over and over again, with a perfectly straight face. (I don't know how they managed that.) We even had to take our best friend along when we went on leave. We did quite a bit of target shooting, even with light machine guns, and I actually did quite well at that. We also stuck bayonets into dummies, threw hand grenades, and crawled under barbed wire.

But most of our time was spent on various work assignments. Here are some that I can remember:

Digging holes for bomb shelters.

Laying railroad tracks.

Working in ordinance stores, clothing depots, food stores.

Unloading railroad cars.

Putting up Nissen huts. (This was the British version of Quonset huts, corrugated iron tunnels.)

The railroad tracks that we laid were to provide a training facility for something that had been used a great deal in the years of trench warfare in WWI, namely heavy railway artillery. In WWII it turned out to be about as anachronistic as the cavalry that our Polish friend in Paris had been so proud of. On that job, several railroad cars full of cinders arrived one day. The cinders had gotten wet and wouldn't fall through the openings at the bottom. So some of us climbed up, poked around with crowbars, and succeeded so well that I too fell right through a hole and emerged from under the car covered with black stuff. The sergeant major ran up to me and asked whether I was O.K.? Like a fool I said yes. I could have had some sort of pain, gone to sick bay, and got at least a day off.

Most of the work on that project, which lasted several months, was with pick and shovel. I was in such good physical condition that after doing that for 8 hours I sometimes played tennis in the evening.

The only other accident I ever had was to drop a heavy iron picket on my foot. The point went through my boot and made a hole in my foot which swelled up quite badly. No bone was broken, but I got several weeks of "light duty" which I hated because it meant peeling potatoes and scrubbing big kettles in the damp kitchen. I would have much preferred to be outside.

Talking about kitchens, there was plenty to eat, not just in the armed forces, but for civilians as well. Some foods were rationed, but the rations were adequate and were always available. According to some reports, the general state of health in England was better during the war than before, in spite of the almost total absence of citrus fruits. Oranges came in occasionally from "neutral" Spain (which had troops fighting alongside the Germans on the Russian front), and more arrived after the Allies controlled French North Africa. Spam, powdered milk and powdered eggs arrived from the U.S., corned beef from Argentina, and one could always get fish and chips.

Bananas were nonexistent. When a comedian wanted a laugh, all he had to do was to say that he had slipped on a banana skin. Any mention of the Italian navy had the same effect. There was quite a bit of entertainment of that sort, plus movies and dances, so life wasn't all work and no play.

During the winter of 1942-43 I was a janitor. Catterick, being a large permanent camp, had quite a bit of family housing and also an elementary school. My job was to go there every morning, well before the crack of dawn, and light fires in 18 iron stoves, one in each classroom. I started with paper and wood kindling and some coal on top of that. When the coal started burning (which sometimes took a while if the wood wasn't dry) I filled the stove with coke, and that lasted all day. I must have had a lot of free time that winter.

The town nearest to Catterick is Darlington, about 12 miles away. In the fall of 1941 I started to go there for evening classes organized by the University of London, in Mathematics, Physics, and Chemistry. (This was the first time that I had a lab course.) In December 1942 I went to London for exams and was awarded a so-called Intermediate B. Sc. This certified that I had successfully completed the first year of a B. Sc. degree.

On leaves I either went to London, which was always interesting, or I visited the Chestertons, the family whom we met in Paramé just before the war. They took me in almost as one of their own. I felt that I had a home away from home with them, something for which I am still grateful. At first they lived in Brighton, on the South coast, and then moved to Hove, next door. London was about an hour away by train and Mr. Chesterton, who worked in a London bank, made that round trip every day. (In spite of all the bombing, rail traffic remained essentially uninterrupted all through the war.) Audrey was in college, and became a teacher. Brenda, who is a few years younger, later became a mathematician and married one, John Hunter of the University of Glasgow.

As I mentioned earlier, my parents and Vera arrived in New York in June 1941. Papa found work at Presto Recording Co., and Mama also started to work, for the first time in her life. Her first job was being a companion to sick old people, which she found quite depressing. Then she worked in a factory making jewelry, and later she became a saleslady at Macy's. That job she rather enjoyed, and she kept it for many years.

In the fall of 1943 Papa was hired by Bell Labs. Among other things, I believe that he worked there on sonar (the acoustic equivalent of radar, used to detect submarines).

We exchanged letters quite frequently. Once, after I told them about a visit to the Chestertons in the summer, they asked whether it had been warm enough to go swimming. I had to explain that because of the nasty people on the other side of the Channel the English beaches were full of barbed wire and mines and possibly other dangerous stuff and that therefore it was not a good idea to go swimming there!

Vera got her high school diploma in June 1942 and then went to Sterling College, a small school in Kansas, on a scholarship. She majored in Chemistry and claimed that she was the unique student there who had never milked a cow.

Mama tried of course very hard to get her parents, who were still in Avignon, out of France. By the end of November 1941 she had got visas to Cuba for them and had even booked their passage from Lisbon, but when they were ready to go, the Spanish border was closed. This was right after Pearl Harbor. I don't know whether this was related to closing the border, nor do I know how long it remained closed. In any case, they abandoned that plan. Mama kept on trying to get U.S. visas for them, and she almost succeeded. In October 1942 they were actually invited to come to the U.S. Consulate in Marseille, but it was too late: on November 11 the Germans occupied all of France (in response to the Allied landings in North Africa) and from then on it was impossible to leave.

I tried to learn more about America (beyond Cowboys and Indians and Al Capone) by reading some history, especially biographies. Even before entering the war the U.S. had helped Britain enormously by lending 50 destroyers. But I also realized that American opinion was not quite unanimous: A few days after the German invasion of Russia, Life magazine ran an article showing pictures of dead Russian soldiers who "had paid the price for resisting the victorious Germany army" (or words to that effect). That article could have come straight out of Berlin.

Which reminds me of my earlier statement that Swiss neutrality leaned in the good direction: Much of the content of the Neue Züricher Zeitung could have come straight out of London.

My best friend at that time was Ernst Landsberg. He had lived in Hanover and Berlin, came to England in 1937, and was cared for by a church group in Essex. His mother was still in Germany, his father in Holland. He had studied social sciences, was interned for a while, and then joined the P.C.

Other good friends were Julius and Gerard. I don't remember their last names. Julius was a medical student, very smart, an irreligious son of a Hamburg rabbi, Gerard came from Vienna; we had known each other on the Isle of Wight in the summer of 1937. The four of us often had very deep discussions on how to solve the really BIG problems, such as how the world should be organized so that there would be no more wars, or how one should go about re-educating the youth of Germany. The latter topic was Ernst's particular concern. He was hoping to return there, after the war, as part of some U.N. outfit.

In 1943, when an Allied invasion of Western Europe was beginning to be a possibility, the Army gave us a chance to change our names. The reason was that an obviously German-Jewish name might be dangerous in case of capture. So, on July 17, 1943, "Army No.: 138040, Rank: Pte., Name: Pollak-Rudin, W., changed his name on Army authority to Army No.: 13053436, Rank: Pte., Name: Rudin, W.". (My parents and Vera also dropped Pollak some time after their arrival in New York.)

Ernst switched from Landsberg to Russell, the name of the man who had been his substitute father for the last 6 years.

At that time, for similar reasons, some educational programs were started in Catterick Camp. I got to teach French to a group of sergeants. This was my first teaching experience. They were absolute beginners, and I don't know whether I managed to teach them very much, but I enjoyed it. Julius did the same with German, and Ernst lectured about Germany, Nazis, resistance movements, etc. We three were obviously the Camp intellectuals!

Toward the end of 1943 the authorities decided that they could trust us a bit more. We were offered a chance to leave the Pioneer Corps and transfer to some other type of military service. I had become very bored with the P.C. but didn't have much enthusiasm for artillery or infantry or tanks (which some of us chose; many stayed in the P.C.). But one day it was announced that the Navy needed interpreters, native German speakers preferred. That sounded much more interesting to Ernst, Gerard, and me. In January we were called to London, for interviews and some tests, were accepted, and joined the Royal Navy on February 4, 1944.

In the U.S. the rivalry between the Services is so ingrained that a transfer from the Army to the Navy seems to be an inconceivable concept for most Americans. At least that is the reaction I get when I tell this story. But in Britain it was not so uncommon to shift people around as needs arose. To mention another example of this flexibility, when more coal was needed and there was a shortage of miners, the draft calls included a lottery which decided who would not perform any military service at all but would work in the mines instead. They were generally regarded as the losers.

CHAPTER 15

Navy

R.N.T.E. Southmead was a house in Wimbledon, large enough to accommodate about 25 trainees (that's what the T stood for) and a couple of instructors. It pretended to be a ship. We "went ashore" in a "liberty boat", got "shore leave" in the evening, the floor was the "deck" and the kitchen the "galley". Anyone coming in "came aboard".

It contained many recordings, realistically scratchy, with a goodly dose of static, of German ship-to-ship radio traffic, plus earphones with which we, the trainees, listened to these recordings, and log books for writing down what we heard. That's what the job was going to be.

We were called "headache operators". (This was near the beginning of that period in our civilization when everything has to have a cute code name, such as Barbarossa or Overlord or Desert Storm.) We knew that we would soon be on destroyers in the Channel and the North Sea, would twirl the dials on our radios till we heard something, and if it was exciting or significant we would call "headache-bridge" into the voice pipe, wait for the answer "bridge-headache" and then give the message.

The war had reached the stage where our air superiority was such that there was essentially no German naval activity in the Channel or the North Sea during the day. But there was quite a bit of action at night, when they tried to attack cargo ships with their so-called E-boats. (I believe that I never knew what the E stood for.) These were very fast small boats that carried nothing but fuel and torpedoes. If they were hit with anything they just blew up or burned. Their crews used ultrahigh radio frequencies to talk to each other. This limited the range of their signals to the horizon, and we were told that we probably wouldn't hear anything unless we were within 6 or 7 miles of them.

After about 3 weeks, barely knowing one end of a ship from the other, we were sent to sea. I drew La Combattante, a Free French destroyer. When I went aboard in Harwich (an East coast port) a man came down a ladder, very casually dressed in a sweater. I asked him where something was that I was looking for, and he answered with a grin: "On ne demande pas ça au capitaine." And that turned out to be typical of this ship: it was very informal, easygoing, relaxed, friendly. The crew was French, with just a few Englishmen for liaison. And this time no one even suggested the Foreign Legion!

Within an hour or so after my arrival we took off toward Portsmouth. When we were in the strait of Dover, which is only about 20 miles wide, German shore batteries fired at us from Calais but missed. One of the shells came close enough that bits of shrapnel hit the ship's side.

We were part of a destroyer flotilla based at Portsmouth. It also included a Polish destroyer, the rest were British. Its main objective was to protect convoys of cargo ships. My working hours were at night because, as mentioned earlier, not much was happening during the day, but actually most nights were also quite uneventful, and boredom was a very real problem.

However, we did sink at least two E-boats in the three months that I spent on La Combattante. Once there were survivors whom we picked up; one of them had fairly detailed information about our convoy in his pocket. The other time we just picked up some bodies.

Since I was the only headache operator on board I had a long night shift and had trouble getting enough sleep. It was hard to find a quiet spot during the day. Once I was in what I thought was a very secluded spot on deck, right under one of the 4-inch gun turrets, when someone decided to have a bit of gunnery practice. The ringing in my ears lasted several weeks.

Usually we spent two or three days at sea, sometimes four, followed by a day or two in Portsmouth, a pleasant town which was full of Navy. Quite often I ran across ex-Pioneer Corps friends in one of many pubs.

On May 27 I got orders to leave La Combattante and to join a cruiser, HMS Enterprise, in Plymouth. I remember writing my parents that this was the first time in who knows how many years that I was sorry to leave a place.

I hadn't been in Plymouth since my arrival from France, almost four years earlier. This time I noticed that it had a beautiful harbor, surrounded by green hills. By the time I arrived, my ship had left for Belfast, in Northern Ireland, and I was told to get on a train to somewhere on the west coast (Liverpool?) from where I could catch a ferry to Belfast. I arrived there in the morning and had a few hours in which to look at the city; I suppose my ship hadn't come in yet.

The most interesting thing I remember about Belfast are the numerous signs which surrounded large areas and proclaimed them to be out of bounds to British military personnel. This was done, I was told, to avoid trouble with the Irish Republican Army. In return for their promise not to interfere with the Navy's use of this important harbor, parts of the city were apparently designated to be theirs.

Ireland stayed neutral. Being able to use their harbors would have been of some help in the fight against U-boats, but the idea of helping England seemed to be more than the Irish could bear. About 35 years later I was invited to Dublin to be on a panel that was to select a candidate from among several applicants for a professorship at University College. One of these was a highly recommended mathematician from Oxford. He was interviewed, but we were told ahead of time that "this job is not going to any Englishman". I was also taken to a small German military cemetery a few miles south of Dublin. German pilots whose planes were hit over the western part of England were apparently instructed to try to reach Ireland rather than become POW's in England, and some did.

Being a cruiser, HMS Enterprise was a much larger ship than La Combattante, with bigger guns, a crew of several hundred, and a full-fledged four-ring Captain in command. As soon as I was on board I was told to see him and several other officers in what looked like a conference room, in order to explain what a headache operator was supposed to do. They were obviously not very impressed but they were polite about it. After all, someone in the Admiralty had sent me. It was I who was impressed with me talking to all that high brass!

Soon after we left Belfast a few days later (it must have been June 2 or 3) we were told what was up: The invasion was on! While we were heading south through the Irish Sea, toward Normandy, Rome was liberated on June 4. The date originally chosen for the invasion was June 5, but because the sea was too rough for the small landing craft, D-Day was postposed to next day.

About 5 a.m. on June 6 I heard a German lookout calmly reporting that he saw so-and-so many ships of such-and-such a type approaching from a certain direction, so-and-so many others somewhere else, etc., with not a trace of excitement or alarm in his voice. After a while he vanished. I spent most of the day listening and the same thing happened over and over again: I would tune in on some German talk, and soon it would vanish. I took this as a sign that they had been eliminated by Allied troops.

I also heard a lot of English from ashore. The British used very stylized brief signals. Some Yanks, however, acted like teenagers on the phone.

The point of our being there was of course to use our big guns to fire on whatever targets the troops wanted to have hit. Occasionally I went up on deck to watch the scene. There were ships of all shapes and sizes as far as the eye could see, there were streams of bombers heading south or east, there were landing craft going toward the beach (I was quite content to stay at sea!) and there were the battleships further out. When their 16-inch guns fired you could see the flash, and shortly thereafter their 2,000 lb. shells sounded like trains going over our heads.

That night – or perhaps it was the next night – I heard a German pilot repeat the coordinates of the spot where he was to drop his bombs. I went into my "headache-bridge" routine. On the bridge they had the appropriate maps, with the German grid system (some kindly soul had stolen them for us) and down the voice pipe came the shout: "Hey, that's us!" I suppose that our antiaircraft gunners were alerted. All I really know is that we were not hit.

Our German maps were just one indication of how difficult it was to keep secrets. I already mentioned the convoy information that we found on an E-boat survivor. They also knew perfectly well that an invasion was coming, but by some miracle they did not know when, nor where. On the other hand, the British Embassy in Stockholm sent daily reports about German ship movements in Norwegian waters, and whenever any German ship left a French port someone sent a signal.

I kept on listening, just couldn't quit. But after 3 days with a total of 5 hours of sleep I conked out.

For the next few weeks we occasionally went to Portsmouth for a couple of days and then returned to the French coast. On June 26 we participated in a 3 hour bombardment of German fortifications in the harbor of Cherbourg. Shore batteries fired back, but moving targets hidden by a smoke screen were apparently hard to hit. No ships were sunk, even though some shell splinter wounded our Captain in the shoulder. We even had a newspaper reporter on board for this event.

It was part of the German strategy to hold on to every harbor to the bitter end, as long as they possibly could, because the fewer harbors the Allies could use, the more difficult it was to supply the advancing armies.

After Cherbourg, things quieted down as far as we were concerned. This gives me an opportunity to describe life on board.

Every sailor had a kit bag for his clothes and other belongings, and a hammock for sleeping in. The hammock was made of heavy canvas, contained a narrow fairly stiff mattress and a blanket, and when tied up looked like a very large sausage. When open and with each end fastened to a hook in the wall (oops! the "bulkhead") it was remarkably comfortable to sleep in, especially when it was parallel to the ship's axis, because then you couldn't feel any rolling (sideways motion).

We were divided into messes. Each mess had about 10 or 12 men in it and sent one to the galley to bring the meals and the rum at noon. This was a tradition which (like most Royal Navy traditions) goes back at least to Admiral Nelson of Trafalgar, or perhaps even to Sir Francis Drake of Armada fame: At noon, come hell or high water, the crew got their rum. (The officers didn't, they could buy drinks in the ward room, but if one was really popular he was sometimes offered some rum by the men.) And you could leave your "tot of rum" on the table and come back a couple of hours later and it would still be there. That was a taboo that was really observed. But leaving anything else of value lie around was severely frowned upon: temptations to steal were bad for the morale.

Of course we were very crowded. There was always someone within a few feet of you. But privacy was respected. One could sit quietly in a corner and read a book – there was even a small library on board.

Or, in my case, one could solve differential equations. I had bought Piaggio's book and was working my way through it. (A few years ago there was a series of articles in the New Yorker by Freeman Dyson, an English mathematical physicist at the Institute for Advanced Study in Princeton, in which he mentioned that he worked every problem in that book as a teenager, and even mentioned the price: 12/6. I went to my shelf to check: my copy also has 12/6 pencilled in.) Although some looked at what I was doing, no one made any funny or snide remarks about it.

At that time I really got to know some working class Englishmen. I had eaten at the same table with some in Catterick, or talked to some on a train, but this was different. I was particularly interested in their politics. Churchill was universally admired as a war leader, and no one was in favor of replacing him as such, but almost all of those who were slightly older than I had very bitter memories of Churchill's role in breaking the general strike of 1926. On that level he was an enemy. Having heard all this I was not surprised when the war hero was voted out of office as soon as the war was won in Europe.

One of the most boring jobs was decoding. It was only done by officers and me. There were several types of codes in use. In the most common one, the messages arrived in groups of 4 digits on a paper tape. The decoder had sheets of random digits and a stencil with windows large enough for 4 digits to show. The first few groups of the message told which sheet to use and where to place the stencil on it. Then you took the tape, put the successive 4-digit groups below the successive windows, subtracted without carrying, read the resulting 4 digits to your neighbor, and he looked it up in a code book of 10,000 entries. Of course if you wanted to send a message you did the same thing in reverse. Since no sheet was used very often it was probably a very secure system, but it was awfully slow. HMS Enterprise was big enough to have a chaplain on board. He had officer rank, but absolutely refused to help with this chore. He claimed that he was a noncombatant, and decoding would endanger his Geneva convention privileges in case of capture. He was not popular with his fellow officers.

Toward the end of July we went to Scapa Flow. This is a large anchorage in the Orkney Islands, north of Scotland, a really desolate place. At least I thought so, I went ashore exactly once in the week that we were there. Then we went to Edinburgh and got a week's leave.

What comes next is sad. I had run into Ernst several times in Portsmouth and I knew that he was on a destroyer, HMS Quorn. In Scapa Flow I had heard that that ship was sunk on August 3, and I was now hoping to see him while he was on survivor's leave. When I phoned Mr. Russell (his adopted father) I heard that he was missing, presumed dead.

It's a funny thing. Intellectually we knew very well that getting killed was always a distinct possibility but somehow it never really registered, even after I had known of the sinking.

At the end of September I was ordered to report to the naval base at Harwich. There I was not attached to any ship, but to a flotilla of ancient smelly cramped destroyers. I just went out on night patrols on whichever one I got assigned to. Gerard did the same thing, and rather than stay in whatever naval accommodations were available ashore we rented a room in town, for very little money. The landlady even did our laundry, and the Navy didn't seem to mind.

There was a Captain in command of the whole flotilla. On his ship, my radio was in his sea cabin in which his bunk was the only place to sit. Once he came in and yelled: "You are sitting on my pants!"

What I remember most about this period is that I got seasick almost every time. The North Sea seemed to be a lot rougher than the Channel. The standard advice, to lie flat on your back and get fresh air, was of course quite useless; there was nothing to do but keep a bucket handy. I was always totally miserable, especially after I had nothing left to throw up, but as soon as I stepped ashore I recovered instantly. And there was another consolation that was frequently offered: Admiral Nelson had also suffered from seasickness.

This assignment lasted only a month, till about Nov. 1, when I was sent to HMS Riou, one of several frigates based at Harwich which had just been built at the Boston Navy Yard. (My naval education never advanced far enough to learn the difference between a destroyer and a frigate.) These ships were much roomier and airier than what I had just been on. We slept in triple bunks, not in hammocks (there were pros and cons to that) and, most important, they were sturdy: almost every ship in this flotilla (not Riou, luckily) ran on a mine some time in the next six months, and every one of them returned to port under her own steam.

This was the first time that I had an "oppo" (opposite number, i.e., a second headache operator), a nice young Englishman called Peter. He had been on the ill-fated Quorn but was sent to an American destroyer before D-Day. Luck is what you needed to have!

Having an oppo obviously meant that I had more time. To correct this, I was appointed to be the ship's mailman.

Except for the skipper and the Petty Officers (it was they who really ran the ship) I was, at $23\frac{1}{2}$, one of the oldest on board. The average age was more like 19.

There were about a dozen New Zealanders among us; about half of them were Maoris, and it was good to see that they were totally at ease with the rest, and vice versa. They received fabulous food parcels from home which we all enjoyed.

By that time, mail to France was functioning again. I wrote to Avignon, to get news from my grandparents, and received a postcard from Apapa which made me suspicious: the bottom half was in his handwriting, the top half pretended to be in Amama's, but it was too firm and even, it looked as if it had been written by a much younger person. I sent the card to Mama, and she realized right away that this was not written by her mother. She wrote this to me, but before I got that letter I was on my way to Avignon!

I had heard, sometime in December, that those who had family in France could apply for leave to visit them. I applied, without asking for any particular length of time, and to my utter surprise I was given six weeks!

CHAPTER 16

Avignon

On January 4, 1945, I left Portsmouth on a boat filled with French civilians which took me to Dieppe, from where I hitched a ride to Paris. Even though it was dark when we arrived (there may still have been a blackout) I recognized the landmarks and found a hotel that had been taken over by the British Army. I must have had the right travel orders to be able to stay there, for free, and to get a train ticket to Avignon a couple of days later.

The best way to describe the next few weeks is to simply reproduce the following report.

14th February, 1945.

Dear Mama, dear Papa, dear Vera,

As this letter is going to be very long and I have a typewriter at my disposal I am addressing it jointly to all three of you and will send a copy to each address. I will try, however, to keep it as short and concise as possible.

1.– AMAMA'S DEATH. Amama died on the 15th of June, 1943. She did not suffer acutely, it seems, towards the end, but fell asleep one evening and did not wake up any more. Of course the very bad food situation at that time was probably the main cause. Apapa himself was very ill than, so ill that he could not even go to the funeral. He did not want you to know about it and kept up the pretence that Amama was still alive. Still, however sad it is, truth must come out eventually in a case like this.

2.– HOW APAPA LIVES. He is still in the same room, and does his own cooking on a small electric heater. While I was there he did not go out at all, it being too cold. There is no heating in the room, so he very often stayed in bed altogether, this being the only warm place, and I did the cooking for him. But he is not ill at all, on the contrary, I think it is quite amazing how he has stood all those hardships for such a long time.

There are two ladies who do all his shopping for him, Mme. Wolff, from Strasbourg, and Mme. Chobaut. More about her later. Cooking consists mainly of soups (oat flakes, bouillon), potatoes, spaghetti, tea. Apapa has a "Regime" ration card and so gets $\frac{3}{4}$ kg sugar, $\frac{3}{4}$ kg pâtes, 6 kg potatoes monthly in exchange for his meat tickets; as well as $\frac{1}{4}$ lt milk daily.

When I left Avignon the weather was already much warmer and I hope he will soon be able again to go out.

3.– PERSONAL CONTACTS. Mme. Henriette Chobaut. Wife of the archiviste at the Palais des Papes. Speaks German and English, paints. Two daughters, 11 and 16. She has been a very great help for Apapa, made his acquaintance through Dr. Jokl. I was there very often, they are very nice and intelligent people. I think you might send her a letter, the address is simply "Palais des Papes, Avignon", telling her how much her help is appreciated.

There are some more people who sometimes come to pay Apapa a visit, but none of them are interesting. There is Mrs. Wolff, and an old lady, Mme. Kahan, who is very religious and tried to convert me to Zionism, Mr. Konrad, a rather shady character in my estimation, former Nazi, then communist. And of course there is the landlady who manages to make a lot of money by "doing favours" to Apapa giving him from time to time some cheese or milk or other food stuffs.

4.– FINANCIAL SITUATION. The $300 which you sent have arrived at the Paris branch of the New York City Bank and $200 have already been received by Apapa, the remaining instalments are to follow. As I did not know that you had been able to send that money I brought Apapa 10,000 frs. He insisted on having all my expenses put to his charge as well and gave me a receipt for $300. In any case, he has now enough money for at least 6 or 8 months, according to his estimation, and does not want you to send him any more before he asks for it. Also Zygfryd should not send any money now.

5.– IMMEDIATE PLANS. As soon as weather and travelling conditions improve Apapa will go to Dr. Reich who has invited him a long time ago. Needless to explain how much better off he would be

there than all alone in his miserable little room. The address is
c/o Bertha Reich, 17, rue de l'obelisque, Marseille. It is "Bertha"
because she is at home more often than he and that is an advantage
when registered mail arrives.

Nothing holds Apapa back in Avignon now as I ordered a stone for Amama's grave and had it set while I was there.
He said he would not have left before that had been done, and as
he does not even go out now God knows when it would have been
done. There was some difficulty in finding the grave as it had not
been marked properly, but I did find it in the end.

Also, as soon as possible he wants to go to a rest
home or a sanatorium to regain his full strength again and some of
his lost weight (20 kg). I would have liked to accompany him to
Marseille, but he won't travel before the end of March.

6.– FUTURE PLANS. Apapa does definitely not want to join you in
America before all his European affairs have been settled. He does
want to join you afterwards! First of all, he intends to go to Vienna
to see whether he can still find any of the things left behind in the
care of Karo Jellinek, both his things and yours, especially all the
silver. For that purpose it will be necessary for you to send him
an authorisation to withdraw the lot in your name, and if possible
the receipt you got with a list of what was deposited. If you can
estimate the value of the various items it would also be helpful in
case of compensation.

Then he plans to go to Bucharest to see what can be
done about Helgea Ltd. He wants to make you, Mama, sole owner
of the shares, which are deposited in a Bucharest bank. By then you
will probably be a U.S. citizen, and should claim compensation from
the U.S.S.R., both for the land and for the stocks taken away during
the first occupation. It is supposed, of course, that the Bucovina will
remain Soviet territory. Apapa thinks that with the company being
registered in Switzerland and you then a U.S. citizen your chances of
success should be good. And even a very small fraction of the value
would be very acceptable. The main work would have to be done
by Apapa himself in Bucharest as he knows all about the business.
Personally I think it is quite possible that the Soviet government
will simply ignore such requests for compensations, but I may be
wrong, let's hope so. In any case Apapa has set his mind to it and
is going to do it.

7.– INFORMATION WANTED. Apapa would like to know whether
Zygfryd and his family intend to stay in Brazil or whether they
plan to return. If Zygfryd comes back he will probably also go to
Bucharest, at least for some time, and they could travel together.
Otherwise, Dr. Reich will be his travelling companion. Also, he
wants to know what Gustl and Natalka plan to do. I will write
them myself, of course, and ask them those questions, but perhaps
you know more about them than I do.

By the way, one can now send letters from England
to France, can one send any from America yet? Apapa was rather
worried when I left him because he had had no news from you for
five weeks. Anyway, it seems that I can communicate better with
him now than you can, so I might pass on messages from you if your
correspondence to France is still restricted.

Apapa would also like to know the state of the account in Zygfryd's name in New York. Is the money you sent him
from that account? When you write him about it, be careful to
mention clearly that it is Zygfryd's account.

8.– PEOPLE YOU KNEW. Mrs. Jokl's address is 18, quai de Brienne,
Toulouse. Her mother has been deported by the Germans, her father
died soon afterwards. Her husband is doctor in a former Vichy
internment camp, but he is free now. She gave me the address of
her brother in London. She works at a Jewish welfare organisation
in Toulouse.

I met Dr. Sauty, who is a friend of Mme. Chobaut's,
being Swiss nothing has happened to him. I also met a friend of his,
M. Sagui, a mathematician who asked me to take some publications
of his (on electronic theories of gravitation and other incomprehen-
sible subjects) to the Davy Faraday Research laboratory in London.

Other people you knew who have been deported are
Mrs. Perlberg and the son of Mrs. Stark.

In Paris I tried to get in touch with M. Givelet, found
one engineer of that name in the telephone directory, address 20, rue
de Laos, rang him up, but he said he did not remember anybody of
your name, I must be looking for some other Engineer Givelet. He
sounded like a rather young man, too. I could not find anyone else
of that name, so don't know what happened to him.

9.– OCCUPATION OF AVIGNON. The Roumanian nationality was a great help when the Germans came. The whole house itself was full of them, but they never bothered the grandparents.

They requisitioned everything they could lay hands on, shot hostages, deported thousands of people, just like everywhere else. One of Apapa's doctors was shot as a hostage. Even now the atmosphere is still poisoned by the memory of the Gestapo, people continuously tell stories of how so-and-so was arrested and how they themselves were not arrested, stories of looting and robbery, and the sad thing it that all those stories are so much alike essentially that they are boring in spite of all the tragedy. I often felt like saying "Can't you talk of anything else now when it is all over?" I suppose it will be the same in all the occupied countries, and even in Germany.

In July 1944 a number of air-raids took place, aiming at the bridges and railways, and they usually hit their targets pretty well. In the inner town, within the ramparts, there is hardly any damage at all. But even so quite a number of people got killed.

There was no fighting for the town during the liberation, the Germans left and the Americans and French arrived later on.

10.– SUPPLIES, FOOD. The food situation is still very bad, due to the difficulties of transport mainly. De Gaulle said in a speech that France used 16000 railway engines before the war, now there are 6000 of which 2/3 are used to supply the armies in the field. The result is irregularity of arrival of supplies, there are notices in the papers whenever anything is to be distributed, e.g. 250 grs maize flour against ticket..., 500 grs sugar against ticket... . The rationing system is complicated and the only food that can be had in approximatemy sufficient quantities is bread (350 grs per day for Apapa's category, more for workers).

In spite of all the efforts to suppress it the black market is still very popular and very expensive. Here are some prices:

1 kg coffee ... 1000 – 1500 Fr	20 cigarettes ... 120 Fr
1 kg butter ... 900 Fr	1 egg .... 20 Fr
1 kg ham ...... 800 Fr	1 tin condensed milk .. 130 Fr

I usually ate in a restaurant at least once a day to give Apapa the benefit of my rations. In Avignon restaurants are

not very expensive, but of course one doesn't get very much either.
Tickets are needed in restaurants too, usually. Prices are about 3-
4 times prewar, at least ("not very expensive"), but can be much
higher too.

I brought some chocolate, sardines, butter, jam,
cheese with me, those were my travelling rations, unfortunately I
did not think of coffee.

Apapa smokes very little now, and says he does not
miss it too much sometimes.

11.– TRAVEL. The railway network has been very badly damaged in
many places, but there is one train daily from Paris to Marseille,
which was very convenient for me. Trains are so crowded that you
can hardly breathe in them, in spite of all the travelling restrictions
(a permit is needed to travel more than 100 km by rail). But if you
travel under U.S. or British orders it is not too bad, I had a reserved
seat every time, more than I would have had in England.

All along the track one can see the wrecks of bombed
and burnt out trains and engines, the destruction must have been
immense.

Something which still belongs to §10 is the cutting
off of electricity during various hours of the day, the reason given
is that the rivers which supply the turbines of power stations are
frozen, and there is no coal to make up for the loss. And some more
about prices: I had the same room that you had (81) for which, I
think, you paid 300 Fr a month. I paid 1500 Fr! Nearly everything
has gone up like that. Apapa still pays a cheaper rate, though.

From the coast to Paris the railways did not yet function, I got a lift by an army car.

12.– EPURATION. That is what the purge of "collaborators" is called.
The trials seem to be fair, as by no means only death sentences
are passed, prison sentences are also used, and some people are
even found not guilty. Many people are sentenced to no more than
"indignité nationale" if the charge is not serious. It seems that the
thing to do for the accused in that case is to burst into tears, whereas
death sentences are received with a shrug of the shoulders. If one
can believe the papers. They are reduced to one half page per issue
now, by the way.

The number of death sentences is still quite large, of course, and the only (very meek) oppsition follows the line "We have seen enough bloodshed, let us have no more, let us try to be one nation of brothers again". That sort of thing can be read in "Figaro", for example, which, with the exception of "Humanité" and "Populaire" is the only prewar Paris newspaper that still exists, I believe.

Sometimes the Maquis take the law into their own hands too. The following happened in Avignon: a number of men armed with tommy guns broke into a prison, kidnapped 12 prisoners, some of whom were serving prison sentences, some of whom were there awaiting their trial, loaded them on a lorry, took them to the river, and shot them. The bodies were later found. Their "executors" probably won't be found, as the search for them is unlikely to be very intensive. Don't take this as typical, though, I am only telling one actual incident.

13.– PORTRAIT OF APAPA. I left him some of your photos, he was very pleased with them. As I cannot send you one of his I will try to describe what he looks like. His hair is quite white (I can't remember whether it was white before the war), and there is very much of it. He is not pale which is surprising when he does not go out. He is much thinner and does not keep himself quite so straight any more. The clothes he wears are rather shabby, but he keeps some for future occasions. He has no chilblains which is very exceptional as nearly everyone has swollen hands, sometimes with deep painful cuts in them. Only his feet hurt him in the cold. On the whole, he has certainly proved that he has a good constitution.

14.– THINGS YOU LEFT IN PARIS. The first attempt to recover some "lost property" started very well. I went to 15, rue Villaret de Joyeuse, 17^e, and asked whether any of your things were still there. I was never more surprised than when the concierge seemed to know all about you, although she had only come in 41. She had been told about you by her predecessor. There is one open suitcase full of junk, one large bag filled with what seem to be woollens or other clothes, and one rather small brown suitcase, so heavy that I could hardly lift it. As none of my keys fitted I opened neither the bag nor that suitcase. Does it contain books? The question is "worth while or not worth while" to send it to you, once that is possible. That is for you to decide, perhaps you only want that suitcase. I left her Apapa's Avignon and Marseille address, and she said she would wait until she hears from us, and then send it wherever we want it. Her name is Mme. R. BERNIER.

15.– END. I am writing this in Paris, during a rainy afternoon. I have to stay here a few days before returning to England, and live a life of luxury. The Hotel Ambassador, Boulevard Haussman, has been requisitioned as a leave hotel by the British Army. There is every comfort, I have a big room with a bathroom, and the best food I have eaten for a very long time. And it is all free.

Apart from that, Paris is not the place it used to be. If one is a millionnaire one can have what one wants, but for the rest of the population life is pretty grim. No buses, no taxis, cutting off of electricity, queues, wooden soles for shoes, usually no heating. But the shops are full of luxury articles, and of course, of photos, paintings, and even sculptures of General de Gaulle, and flags of the Allies. Places of entertainment are handicapped by the restrictions on electric current.

Well, I did not keep my promise to keep this as short as possible, I hope I have not forgotten anything of importance, I don't think I have, and I hope you have been interested in everything I wrote. I am very glad that I had a chance to come here, I really enjoyed it and had an interesting and instructive time.

So long, and all the best,

Walter

Apapa did not have enough time left for any of his plans. Less than two months after I left him he died peacefully, on April 6, 1945, still in Avignon. He was almost 81. Mme. Chobaut sent me a long letter, describing his last days.

While writing this in 1992 I reread that letter. The postcard that had puzzled me in the fall of 1944 happened to be also in front of me. Comparing the handwriting it became clear who had impersonated Amama!

CHAPTER 17

War's End

The first thing I heard when I reported back in Portsmouth was that it had all been a mistake: the family leave granted to me was intended for French citizens only! Of course there was nothing anyone could do about it now, except to admit that bureaucratic foul-ups can occasionally do some good.

I promptly rejoined HMS Riou. By that time Antwerp had been liberated. It was the largest port that could be used to ship supplies to the Allied armies, and most of our night patrols were therefore along the Belgian coast. We spent many a day rolling at anchor off Ostende but unfortunately never got shore leave there. When the weather was rough, lying at anchor close to shore was worse for those of us who were prone to seasickness than being out on the open sea.

Usually some E-boats would leave the Dutch coast at night, carrying mines to the approaches to Antwerp. From their talk I could tell when they actually dropped these mines, and our radar showed where they were at that moment. (Since my station was right next to the navigator's it was easy for us to share information as well as a bucket.) So next morning the minesweepers could go directly to the right spots and dispose of the mines. This game went on for several weeks and apparently it never occurred to the Germans that anyone might be listening. Was it ignorance, or was it arrogance? (At that time they didn't have much to be arrogant about anymore.)

Once we picked a German out of the water who kept saying something about "the power of uranium" and how it would change the war. We had no idea what he was talking about, and I still don't know, because according to all I have read about the subject, German physicists worked on atomic power but not on atomic weapons.

By April it was clear that the war was essentially won, but what surprised me, and perhaps many others as well, was how suddenly it ended. In view of the tenacious German defense of every harbor it seemed quite plausible that part of their army and navy would cling to Norway and that another invasion would be needed. An even more likely possibility was that large numbers of fanatic SS troops would retreat into the Bavarian or Austrian Alps where they might hold out for a long time. After all, their "thousand year Reich" was only 12 years old. What actually happened instead was that lots of highly placed Nazis weren't all that fanatic but had carefully prepared their escapes to South America.

Anyway, a week after Hiltler's suicide it was all over: VE-Day was on May 8, 1945. (VE = Victory in Europe.)

I did not get to London to participate in the celebration that day because our ship stayed on patrol, for just in case, I guess.

About three weeks later we were sent to Hamburg. We were the first Allied ship to enter that harbor. At the mouth of the Elbe – about 50 miles from Hamburg – we took a German pilot aboard to guide us up the river. He seemed perfectly at ease, needed no interpreter, and even joked: "If we run on a mine, don't blame me, it was your planes that dropped them."

I don't know what the Admiralty's purpose was in sending us there, other than to show the flag, but to me this visit was my real VE celebration. Perhaps the best moment was right at the start, when a group of us walked down the gangway after tying up at a pier. Some German civilians stood around, looking at us, and I heard one say angrily "... und das hat den Krieg gewonnen!" (... and that won the war!).

It seemed absolutely clear to me what he meant: Our bearing was not sufficiently military to suit him, we didn't even march, we were just a bunch of guys walking along. Insult added to injury!

The city was almost flattened. From some points one could see for miles. I have no idea how many people were killed there by air raids, but their shelters must have been very effective because lots of people were up and about and (in marked contrast to what I had seen in France three months earlier) they all looked healthy and very well fed. (Naturally, they had plundered practically all of Europe for the past five years.) After Warsaw, Rotterdam, Coventry, etc., quite apart from the death camps, it pleased me mightily to see a German city that had suffered the same fate.

I realize that such sentiments are politically totally incorrect in 1992, but must everyone be totally PC?

Before going ashore each of us got a pistol. I suppose we also had some ammunition. Since I had never fired a pistol in my life it was fortunate that there was absolutely no need for any weapons. Except for the one guy at the pier, all the natives that I saw were sickeningly friendly. We were not supposed to "fraternize", whatever that meant, but some of us found a bar that was operating, and of couse I talked to people. There was no sign of hostility or animosity. To none of them had it apparently occurred that Germany was guilty of anything, or even that others might think so. "Yes, there was a war, and we lost it, and look how we suffered, but now it's over and we are friends again, aren't we, and you won't let any Russians come here, will you?" They all knew some terrible things that the Russians had done, and were really scared.

And of course no one was or ever had been a Nazi. Which reminds me of a difference between Germans and Austrians: If you asked a German in 1945 whether he had been a Nazi he said: no. An Austrian, asked the same question, said: no, but my neighbor, Herr Meier, he was.

We stayed in Hamburg about 4 or 5 days. On one of these some of us travelled by "duck" (an amphibious truck) to Brunsbüttel, a navel base at the Western end of the Kiel Canal, where we got our first good look at some E-boats. As I mentioned earlier, they burned or blew up as soon as any shot hit them, and none had therefore been captured.

When we returned to Harwich I was ordered back to R.N.T.E. Southmead, where all headache operators were gathering. Our principal concern was of course: when would we be demobilized? There was a formula which produced a priority number depending on age and length of service, but no one knew what this would mean in terms of weeks or months. And there still was the war against Japan.

To keep us busy, we were given German documents to translate. Almost all of these dealt with ship building or engines. There were no engineers among us, we didn't understand the German technical terms, our dictionaries gave us at best a vague idea of what the corresponding English terms might be, and our output must therefore have been totally useless garbage.

I recall only two documents that were mildly interesting to me. One, written before a Japanese delegation was to visit a German naval base, listed the installations that they should see and also those that they definitely should not see. The other, about the Allied landing in Salerno (Italy), included some very clear aerial photographs of the ships as they approached the beach.

To pass the time, I also signed up for two correspondence courses, one in some sort of elementary analysis, and one in projective geometry.

I made no attempt to be admitted to a British university. I had a visa application pending at the U.S. Consulate in London, and since the rest of my family was there I thought it would be best if I joined them as soon as that could be done.

In June Churchill and the Conservative party lost the general election. In August there was Hiroshima and Nagasaki and VJ-Day. And at the end of September we got word that all headache operators would be demobilized right away, regardless of individual priority numbers. We must have had a good friend in the Admiralty!

It took a few days to go through the various "dispersal routines" that were required in order to become a civilian again, a status which I achieved on Oct. 8. Part of the package was eight weeks "resettlement leave" which meant that we still got paid and were still entitled to wear our uniforms.

A colleague, Walter Lewy, had a wife in England but his parents were in New York. We decided to see whether we couldn't spend our leave there. It took us four days, going from one Admiralty office to another, until we found someone who was willing to write "This rating has permission to spend his resettlement leave in U.S.A." on the backs of our demobilization certificates, add an appropriate stamp, and, most important, arranged transportation: for 25 pounds we got passage on the former French luxury liner "Ile de France" which had been converted to a troop ship. We left Southampton on Oct. 15, with several thousand Canadian soldiers, bound for Halifax.

When we arrived there about 5 days later we decided to try to get to New York fast by hitching a ride on some Canadian Air Force plane (there was an airfield in Halifax.) I don't know what gave us the idea that this might work. It didn't, so next day we started on a long slow train trip. When we reached Vanceboro, Maine, in the middle of the night, the U.S. Immigration Inspector hardly looked at us (that's where the uniforms certainly helped), and I sent a telegram to my parents: "Home this afternoon, Walter". (I had written them about being demobilized, but had not said anything about trying to see them since I didn't want to raise false hopes in case something went wrong.)

When my telegram arrived, Papa decided not to go to work that day. Instead he went to Grand Central Station and met every train from Boston, waiting for me to step off. However, I had looked at a map of New York City and had noticed that the 125th Street station was nearer to my parents' address (52 W 91 Street) than Grand Central, so I got off at 125th Street and took a taxi "home". Mama was there, and when Papa phoned that he hadn't found me, I could tell him that I had arrived.

CHAPTER 18

Duke University

It was $5\frac{1}{2}$ years since we had last been together, so we had a lot to talk about.

To make the reunion complete, Vera came up from Durham, North Carolina, where she was a Chemistry graduate student at Duke University. A few days later I accompanied her back to Duke, just to see what an American university looked like. But after talking to some professors in the Mathematics Department and finding out that I already knew most of the material in their undergraduate courses, I thought, why not try to become a student here? They were still on an accelerated wartime schedule, three semesters per year, and one was about to begin.

So I marched into Dean Herring's office (I was still in my Navy uniform, very sure of myself, perhaps obnoxiously so) and announced that I wanted to enroll as a student and that I knew enough Mathematics to get a B.A. degree within a year. Only much later did I realize how preposterous this was from his point of view. He tried to explain that for a degree one needed so many credits, one needed grade point averages, distribution requirements had to be satisfied, stuff that I had never heard of. He also muttered something about perhaps trying the University of Chicago which had a more flexible program. Not realizing that deans were powerful people who could even make department chairmen quake in their boots I kept arguing with him. Finally he agreed to admit me with Junior standing, on probation, subject to my providing copies of my Oxford School Certificate and my London Intermediate B. Sc., and of course subject to my getting good grades at Duke. Which seemed most reasonable to me.

There still was another problem: I had no U.S. visa of any sort. When I left England I had fully intended to return at the end of my leave (I had even rented a room in London) and to wait there for a proper U.S. visa, or to stay there and try to get into a British university. But since I now had contacts at Duke I went with my parents (they

101

guaranteed financial support) to an Immigration Office in New York and asked whether I could stay. To my amazement the answer was yes.

I don't remember whether they gave me a student visa or whether it was called something else. I was told to register with the local draft board as soon as I got back to Durham. This I did, but I was quite determined not to get drafted. I didn't regret or begrudge the time, efforts, boredom, and hardships that I had gone through (mine were of course negligible compared to those suffered by millions of others) – I was even proud to have contributed a tiny bit to winning the war that had to be won – but I felt that six years was enough. I was going to sit the next one out if I possibly could.

Not being a citizen, I could legally refuse to be drafted, but at the risk of being deported and perhaps never readmitted. As it turned out, I was never called.

There was only one luxury that I wanted at Duke: a single room. I had spent too many years too close to too many other bodies. I got one, in one of the dorms on the Main Campus, a rather attractive collection of fake gothic buildings constructed in the late 1920's. There was also an East Campus which contained the women's dorms. Between the two there was about a mile of no-man's-land.

The male students came in two flavors: the veterans and the kids. The latter were more interested in fraternities, which were highly visible and active on Campus, but the former were also liable to be "rushed". My one and only invitation came from ZBT, the Jewish fraternity. (Religion was noted on University documents.) I went, saw that the only purpose seemed to be to drink more beer faster than the next guy, had a few beers and then walked out, never to be asked again. The fact that no other fraternity contacted me didn't bother me, but it make me wonder.

Indeed, some "genteel" forms of antisemitism existed in the U.S. For example, I learned later that some hotels and resorts used "churches nearby" as a code word for "Jews not welcome". Papa and a friend of his, Dr. Kohn, once decided to test this. They asked for a reservation at such a place, putting the two letters in the same mailbox at the same time. Papa got his (he had used Columbia University stationary) and Dr. Kohn was told that the hotel was booked up.

In New York people had warned me that I might have some difficulty in North Carolina with the Southern language, but it wasn't so. True, I was puzzled when I saw "white" and "colored" drinking fountains in a store (did one of them dispense colored water?) but the only linguistic problem that I can remember from that time occurred at the beginning of my Advanced Calculus course. Prof. Elliot was discussing infinite series and kept talking about the use of n. It took me a couple of weeks to realize that he was saying u-sub-n. He must have been an attentive teacher because he saw very soon that the course was too easy for me and suggested that I read parts of Goursat's "Cours d' Analyse" instead. Which I did.

My only academic difficulty was in Chemistry; I had signed up for a quantitative analysis lab. course for which I was woefully unprepared. I made up for that in Physics, where my familiarity with the metric system so impressed the powers that be that I was made a Lab Instructor in the summer of 1946.

That was my first paid teaching job. I also earned some money tutoring football players in trigonometry, and once got $100 for translating some German mothball patents which someone in Durham had obtained from the U.S. Alien Property Custodian. (This translation must have made even less sense than the ship-building literature that we had cranked out in Wimbledon.)

Papa sent me $50 a month until I finished the requirements for my B.A. in Jan. '47, pretty close to the prediction I had made to Dean Herring; this included 6 credits in Religion without which it was totally impossible to get a Duke B.A. in those days.

He had left Bell Labs in March '46, at which time he was hired by the Columbia University Physics Department as their "head gadgeteer". Of course this was not his official title, but it is a pretty accurate job description. They were building one of the first large cyclotrons (in Tarrytown, on the Hudson River) and wanted someone who could quickly design and construct instruments to measure or monitor or stabilize things whenever the need arose. He enjoyed this work very much and was highly appreciated by the whole group. He also took many photographs that recorded the progress of the construction.

Having completed the requirements for a B.A. I followed the path of least resistance and stayed at Duke as a teaching assistant, working toward an M.A. and eventually a Ph.D. During part of that time Vera and I had an apartment in town. (Incidentally, Durham was one of the least attractive towns I had every been in. Especially in summer the whole place stank of tobacco and it was so hot and humid that I put a towel under my arm when I wrote something, so the paper wouldn't get wet.) When she finished her M.A. and went to Ohio State to get a Ph.D. in Biochemistry I moved back to the dorm.

In addition to course work, getting an M.A. (which I did in August '47) involved writing a Masters Thesis. My advisor, John Gergen, suggested that I look through the literature, find as many examples as I could of continuous functions whose Fourier series did not converge everywhere, and describe the various methods of constructing such functions in an intelligible and readable essay. Antoni Zygmund's book "Trigonometrical Series" (known as the analysts' bible in those days) provided enough references to get started. I had it checked out from the library and under my pillow for almost three years.

Note to nonmathematical readers. From now on there will be occasional paragraphs with some mathematical content and with words whose meaning you don't know. Don't let this bother you. Either skip those paragraphs or, better yet, read them and see whether you don't get some idea of what is going on.

There were about 10 or 12 graduate students in Mathematics. All graduate courses were taught by four men: Gergen (harmonic analysis), Thomas (differential equations), Carlitz (number theory, algebra) and Roberts (point set topology). They were all extremely nice to me but not to each other. They were in their forties (and therefore looked like old men to me); they had arrived around 1930, right after Mr. Duke's tobacco money had converted little Trinity College to a full-blown University. Gergen was chairman, the sort of chairman who delegates nothing and tells everyone what to do and how to do it and when to do it. Thomas thought that he ought to have a turn at being chairman and claimed that he was a better mathematician. (He may have been right.) Thomas was jealous of Carlitz because it was "so easy" for Carlitz to write so many papers. Carlitz accused Gergen and Thomas of antisemitism, but I never saw any sign of this. Roberts was the only one who was on good terms with all the others. It was weird.

In the spring of '47, while I was working on my M.A. thesis, something very unpleasant happened. A letter arrived from the Immigration Service, informing me that the visa given to me in Nov. '45 had expired, and that I was about to be deported if I didn't leave the U.S. voluntarily.

My parents knew a lawyer who specialized in immigration problems. With his guidance and advice it took three years of delaying tactics and of applying for this, that, and the other, to make me a legal permanent resident. It was a strain, and it bothered me. I will describe the happy ending when we get to it.

In the fall of '47 I began to work on a Ph.D. thesis. Gergen had me start by studying Chap. XI in Zygmund's book, dealing with uniqueness theorems for trigonometric series. Analogous work had been done for various other systems of functions, but only in one variable, as far as I could find out. I decided to try this problem for series of spherical harmonics. In the one-variable setting, properties of convex functions played a key role. This meant that I needed to find a good analogue of convexity for functions defined on the surface of a sphere. After a few unsatisfactory attempts I was led to reinvent the notion of subharmonicity (without giving it a name). When I found that F. Riesz had proved all the basic properties of subharmonic functions 20 years earlier I felt that I was on the right track. My final results were very similar to the best that were known in the classical case.

I presented this at an AMS meeting at Duke, in April '49. Soon after an abstract of this talk appeared in print, I received an envelope from Zürich, containing a paper published in 1919 by Plancherel, a mathematician who had proved the most fundamental theorem about Fourier transforms. The paper he sent me dealt with the same problem that I had worked on! Fortunately, his results were much weaker than mine, he had to make stronger assumptions, so that the desired conclusions were only proved for a much smaller class of series. (He had preceded Riesz while I had followed him.)

Now here is the point of all this: Had I known of Plancherel's paper, I would probably have been discouraged from tackling this problem. If this famous man could only get such weak results, what am I doing here? Sometimes a little ignorance is a good thing.

The summer of 1948 I spent with my parents. I think that this was my only stay in New York that lasted more than a week or two. Papa had a car by then which we used to get out of town on weekends or for an occasional week. One of their favorite destinations was a small hotel on Lake Hopatkong in New Jersey. And of course I worked on my thesis. It was sufficiently under control by November that Gergen offered me an Instructorship for 1949/50, at a salary of $3,500 and a teaching load of 12 hours per week. It sounded fine to me and I accepted.

My parents came to Duke for Commencement in June '49. They both enjoyed meeting my professors and fellow students, and Papa enjoyed talking about extrasensory perception with Dr. Rhine. A couple of months earlier I had bought an ancient Buick for $100 from one of the Assistant Deans. He warned me that the car was OK for local use, but that he wouldn't try to drive it to New York, for instance. Which is of course exactly what I was planning to do, with my parents as passengers. The car had trouble climbing uphill because the fuel pump was defective, and the radiator occasionally boiled over, and somewhere in Virginia (after we had spent a few days in Virginia Beach) there was a loud clanking noise and the engine died. I managed to coast down to a garage. When I told the mechanic that I thought there was something loose under the hood he reached in and came up with a broken piece of crankshaft! For some reason he gave me $40 for the wreck. We got on a bus to Washington, saw the sights, conferred with the Washington associate of my lawyer, and continued to New York by train.

When the next academic year started in September I saw that the Mathematics Department (i.e., Gergen) had hired another new Instructor. She was Mary Ellen Estill, a very attractive young lady who had just got her Ph.D. at the University of Texas, and who later became my wife, the mother of our four children, a famous set-theoretic topologist, and a grandmother of our three grandchildren. (I was a bit slow in proposing marriage, but I did get around to it eventually, as you will see if you read on.)

The two of us and a few others who were low in the pecking order had offices that were little cubicles in a former classroom. They were separated by thin walls that were only about 6 feet high. My first act of gallantry was to climb over one of these into Ellen's cubicle; she had left her key inside and was locked out.

We both lived on East Campus that year, she in a graduate dorm for women, I in a house called the Faculty Annex which was occupied only by males. We saw each other a lot and enjoyed it.

The annual December AMS meeting was at Columbia University that year. There I met Zygmund for the first time, and gave a 10-minute paper to which Papa listened. He said afterwards that he had understood every word but not a single sentence!

In January 1950 my immigration problem was about to be solved. My lawyer knew of a procedure called pre-examination, which meant that instead of leaving the U.S. and applying for an immigration visa at some U.S. Consulate I could do the applying while staying in the country. This had something to do with some legislation concerning displaced persons. When all the papers had been properly shuffled and the visa granted I still had to go to a Consulate for final approval.

So, on Jan. 31 I travelled to Montreal, armed with a piece of paper that promised the Canadians that even if something were to go wrong at the Consulate I would be allowed to come back to the U.S.

In the morning of Feb. 1 I had my interview with the Consul. All went well until he asked for my passport in order to stamp the visa into it. When I told him how I had ripped it up and thrown it in a ditch 10 years ago, he sent me out to phone the Austrian Consulate in Ottawa and ask for a new Austrian passport. I did, and was refused instantly for a reason that seemed totally idiotic to me: I was not a resident of Canada. When I returned with that absurd story I was sure the Consul wouldn't believe me and would just throw me out. But he accepted it as quite natural that not being a Canadian resident was a perfectly logical reason for not getting an Austrian passport, dictated an "Affidavit in lieu of Passport" to a secretary which explained the situation, attached my picture, had me sign it, and put the visa stamp on it. Amazing!

Soon after I got back to Durham I celebrated my new status by buying a brand-new Ford.

Gergen had already done a lot for me, and that spring he did me one last big favor: he urged me to go elsewhere. I was very ignorant of what went on in other universities. In particular, I didn't realize that the Duke Mathematics Department didn't compare all that well with many others. Following his suggestion I applied for a Bell Telephone Fellowship which he saw advertised, and for a 2-year Research Instructorship at M.I.T., the Massachusetts Institute of Technology. I didn't get the first (it was awarded to a logician, Lisl Gal, another ex-Viennese, and I don't remember what the benefits would have been) but I did get the M.I.T. job which was almost certainly the better of the two.

So I packed my stuff in the trunk of my car at the end of the semester, said good-bye to all my good friends, and headed North to Cambridge, Mass.

CHAPTER 19

M.I.T.

My new job was called a C.L.E. Moore Instructorship. This was a nonrenewable two-year position with a reduced teaching load of 6 hours per week to which two new instructors were appointed each year. It was only about 3 or 4 years old, and I believe that I was the first recipient who had not got his Ph.D. from either Harvard or Princeton or Chicago. I don't know how I got so lucky. I suspect that Zygmund may have written a letter about me – he was the Analysis editor of the Transactions of the AMS when I submitted my thesis for publication there, and he had sent a nice note about it to Gergen.

The Department's star was of course Norbert Wiener, but there were lots of other first-rate people, all extremely friendly and willing to talk to a beginner like me. Those with whom I had contact included Norman Levinson, Witold Hurewicz, George Whitehead, Ambrose, Dirk Struik, Ted Martin, Stefan Bergman, Raphael Salem. (Non-mathematicians: please forgive the name-dropping.) Among the graduate students I formed lasting friendships with Allen Shields, Harold Shapiro, John Nohel, Jake Levin.

But the person there who influenced me the most was Iz Singer. He and I were the two Moore Instructors hired that year. He was a Chicago Ph.D. and knew enormously more Mathematics than I. (What I had learned at Duke I had learned well, but there were large areas that had never been mentioned there.) The most important thing was not any particular facts that I learned from him, it was his way of thinking about Mathematics, of looking at problems, of relating one field to another. He is now best known for the Atiyah-Singer index theorem.

One of my first assignments was to teach a Junior-Senior type course which was probably called "Advanced Calculus" although "Analysis" may have been part of its title. This was an excellent class. For example, the only sophomore in it, Louis de Branges, later settled the Bieberbach conjecture.

When I complained to Martin (the Department Chairman who also happened to be a consulting editor for McGraw-Hill) that there was no good book that contained the topics to be covered, he said "Why don't you write one?" I never found out whether he was kidding or not, but I started to write while I taught the course from my notes. After I sent an outline and a sample chapter to McGraw-Hill they offered me a contract. I completed the manuscript for "Principles of Mathematical Analysis" in the spring of 1952. The book was published in 1953, is still widely used 39 years later, is in its third edition, and exists now in at least 15 languages.

When I wrote it my purpose was to present a beautiful area of Mathematics in a well-organized readable way, concisely, efficiently, with complete and correct proofs. It was an esthetic pleasure to work on it. That it turned out to be so popular was a welcome additional bonus.

I listened to courses given by Wiener, Salem, and Ambrose, and of course went to seminars. In one of these we struggled with the theory of distributions – Laurent Schwartz' book had just appeared.

I lived in a room with bath, on Brewster Street, near Harvard Square. The landlady, Mrs. Galacar, mentioned occasionally that she had been excommunicated. I never had what it took to ask her what she had done to deserve such an honor. I owned a hot plate, a coffee pot, one plate, one cup, one fork, ..., obviously not enough to do any serious cooking. But a nearby Chinese restaurant served dinner for 65 cents.

There were summer picnics on Crane's Beach (north of Boston) where the water was always cold but one could eat lobsters cooked right there on the beach, there were several international clubs around for entertainment, and one could sail on the Charles River, in M.I.T. – owned boats. Ruth Goodwin, the Department Secretary, was my sailing instructor. I never capsized, but I could see Mass. General Hospital on the other side of the river and was going to rush right over to be decontaminated in case I did. The river was none too clean.

To my surprise I received a job offer from Cornell in the spring of 1951 after I gave a talk there. I liked the place very much but declined the offer, because I hated to give up my second year at M.I.T. It didn't occur to me to ask whether Cornell would hire me with the understanding that I would only show up a year later. That sort of arrangement is now fairly common. I don't know what the reaction would have been then.

In the summer of 1951 I drove West, zigzagged through Colorado, New Mexico, Utah, and Wyoming for about 6 weeks, ending up in Minneapolis at the annual summer meeting of the AMS. Ellen was there – and in fact, for the next couple of years, AMS meetings were where we used to meet.

Being relatively close to New York I saw my parents quite often. I remember two vacation trips with them during that time, one to Bar Harbor, Maine, the other to Cape Cod.

Turning back to the summer of 1950, that's when the Korean War started, just as I arrived in Cambridge. It had hardly any impact on our lives at M.I.T. (and no one invited me to contribute my military expertise to that cause), but Mc Carthyism was in full swing. Anticommunism had become the state religion of the U.S. and heretics were given a hard time. One member of the Department, Dirk Struik, a Marxist one of those main interests was the history of Mathematics, was indicted, not by the House Unamerican Activities Committee or any other U.S. agency, but by the Commonwealth of Massachusetts, for advocating the overthrow of said Commonwealth! M.I.T.'s reaction was to suspend him, fortunately with pay. (Once a professor was accused, it was unthinkable to expose innocent young students to such a dangerous person.) The case was dropped, after a year or so, for lack of evidence.

This was the age of the loyalty oath. Many universities insisted that all faculty members must sign one. At Berkeley, several professsors resigned over this issue; they were eventually hired back when politics returned to normal. I don't remember any fuss about an oath at M.I.T., but I did receive such a form to sign once, asked whether it applied to me since I wasn't a citizen, and never heard about it again. A few years later, when I was in Rochester, a letter came from the University of Oklahoma, offering me a position there; included was a loyalty oath form, to be signed before they would speak to me any further. My circular file was conveniently close.

One evening, early in 1952, Singer and I were in the Whitehead's basement, watching a ping-pong game, when he asked me a question: If A is an algebra of continuous functions on the closed unit disc which contains the identity function, and if the absolute value of every member of A attains its maximum on the boundary of the disc, must every member of A then be an analytic function?

Next morning I knew that the answer was yes.

I got tremendous satisfaction from this. My thesis had been a good piece of work, technically quite difficult, but not all that original; it had followed a trail that had been around for quite some time. Some of the papers I had written since then were variations on the same or similar themes, o.k. but not exciting. But this was different. It was a new kind of theorem, and, to make things even better, it had a short simple proof that one could immediately understand, without painful line-by-line checking.

Singer raised the question because he was interested in finding analytic structures in spectra of Banach algebras. I regarded the theorem as a characterization of analyticity in which the maximum modulus property plays the major role. It made me feel that I really was a mathematician.

The paper in which this and some related results appear (Duke Math. J., vol. 20, 1953) contains a marvelous misprint on p.450.

Academic jobs were in short supply in the spring of 1952. I sent about 15 applications (nowadays Xerox makes it so easy that students send 300) which yielded two interviews, at the University of Maryland and the University of Rochester. At the latter, after my lecture on maximum modulus algebras, I was asked: "How do you find such theorems?" I don't know how I answered, but I should have said: "You need to have someone like Singer around, to ask the right questions!"

Rochester appealed to me more than Maryland, and I accepted their offer of an Assistant Professorship.

CHAPTER 20

Rochester

The campus of the University of Rochester was on the southern edge of town, near the Erie Canal, wedged between the Genesee River and a large cemetery. During my first year there I sublet an apartment just across the river in a group of three buildings that once had been an orphanage.

The Mathematics Department was small, not active researchwise, but a nice friendly group of people. Its chairman, John Randolph, had written a calculus book with Mark Kac which was too good to be widely used. (Widely used calculus books must be mediocre.) Ralph Raimi was the other new arrival that fall. We still see each other occasionally and are good friends.

In June 1953 I spent two weeks at the University of Michigan, for a Complex Analysis conference. Being on the same program with Ahlfors, Kakutani, Bochner, and having my talk scheduled immediately after Nevanlinna's, was a bit unnerving, but I guess I did all right. Someone handed me $25 afterwards, as an honorarium. I was surprised because money had not been mentioned at all.

That spring, when Ellen and I had met in New York, we had made plans for me to visit her in Houston where she was going to spend the summer with her family. So as soon as the conference was over I pointed my car south, toward Texas.

Her parents – everyone called them Pop and Irene – gave me a very warm welcome. Pop – who was really Joe Jefferson Estill – was a civil engineer who had recently retired from the Texas Highway Department and was now working for a private company. Just before the Depression hit he had been sent to West Texas to survey and eventually build a road through the Frio valley. But then there was no money to build, so surveying was all he could do for many years, and the Highway Department just left him there.

Almost all of Ellen's childhood (she was born on Dec. 7, 1924) was thus spent in Leakey, a "town" of about 100 people, which she always describes with great enthusiasm as a wonderful place for a kid to grow up in. Her high school class had 4 students in it, and she entered the University of Texas at the age of 16.

A few days after my arrival in Houston, and after we had been to the Galveston beach a couple of times, I decided that the time had come to pop the question. Ellen didn't say yes instantly, but it didn't take her very long, and that evening we announced at dinner that we were going to get married. Pop seemed pleased, Irene looked a little dubious for a few minutes, but then she began to plan the details of the wedding. (She turned out to be an excellent mother-in-law and an absolutely fabulous grandmother.) For the next few days I met large numbers of relatives, in Houston as well as in and near Grapevine (between Dallas and Fort Worth) where Pop had a lot of family. There we stayed with Aunt Kate, Pop's older sister, an impressive old lady.

And then I was sent away. The wedding was set for August 19, and it was evidently thought to be quite improper and possibly immoral for me to hang around my fiancee all that time. So I drove off to Colorado for a few weeks and hiked around the Rocky Mountain National Park and other places.

My parents decided not to come to the wedding. They had never flown, and Houston just seemed too far from New York to go there by train. But Vera and her busband, Earl Usdin, drove down from Levittown near Philadelphia to give me some moral support. (Earl was a biochemist. He and Vera had been fellow students at Ohio State where they got their Ph.D's.)

A few days before the wedding we had tea with the minister who was going to perform the ceremony in the Estill backyard. I expected him to inquire into my religious background, beliefs, etc., but I think all we talked about was the weather and other equally safe topics.

At the wedding, Vera was the bridesmaid and Joe, Ellen's brother, was best man. We spent a 4 or 5 day honeymoon in Galveston, then came back to Houston, squeezed all our wedding presents into my car, and started on the long trek to Rochester. (One of Pop's brothers, Uncle Pete, had given me a new set of tires as a much appreciated wedding present.)

Our first major stop was Winchester, Tennessee. This is where the Estills and the Shooks had lived for many generations. Some Estills had moved to Texas, where Pop was born, but he went back to Winchester to marry Irene Shook. She had three sisters, Lora, Kathryn, and Sally, as well as a brother, Allen, all still living there. We stayed with Lora. She was the oldest, was a widow, and was clearly the head of the family. Her husband had run a profitable tutoring school for rich Yalies in New Haven, while she had stayed in Tennessee and managed a farm. This remainded me very much of how Apapa and Amama lived in two places, Vienna and Hilcze. I don't know how old Lora was, she was almost immobile, but she cooked fantastic meals, including fresh fried chicken for breakfast!

Kathryn experimented with plants in a greenhouse, Allen ran a hardware store, Sally was married to Will who tried to sell me insurance and whose five year old grandson was allowed to wave shotguns around. That kid make me nervous.

From there we went to Durham, to surprise some of our old friends with our new status. Ellen was not scheduled to teach at Duke during 1953/54, she had an NSF grant to spend the year at the University of Michigan. (It was very nice that this grant could be transferred to Rochester.)

Next came a visit to Vera and Earl, and then we went on to Tennanah Lake in the Catskills where my parents were vacationing and waiting to meet their new daughter-in-law. We spent a happy week with them before driving on to Rochester.

I had a small apartment in the same ex-orphanage in which I had spent the previous year. It was in the attic, one could not stand up in the bathtub, but we managed to fit in. The U. of R. was very nice to us: Ellen got a part-time appointment, on very short notice. A few months before our first baby was expected we moved to a larger apartment, in what had been the auditorium of the orphanage. It had a 2-story living room and a bedroom overlooking it.

Catherine was born on July 17, 1954. All four grandparents came almost instantly to admire their grandchild. This was their only meeting ever. I think that each couple had been a bit apprehensive about meeting the other, and they were all on their best behavior.

Six weeks later we put Catherine into a basket that fit snugly on the front seat between the two of us and drove to the AMS meeting in Laramie, Wyoming. Those meetings were much smaller than they are now, we knew most of those who came, they were almost like large family gatherings.

My teaching load was the standard 9 hours per week. This left me plenty of time to do a lot of good mathematics in those years, some of it on our fire escape which we used as a balcony. In the spring of 1955 the Department recommended two promotions, one for me and one for another guy who had been there much longer. Dean Hoffmeister thought that one promotion was enough and that seniority was more important than research. But just then Washington University in St. Louis offered me an associate professorship with a big jump in salary. The dean immediately changed his mind and even raised my salary beyond the offer. Just like in a poker game!

Having got tenure and feeling rich we immediately bought an old somewhat run-down high-ceilinged 4 bedroom house. The address was 64 Brighton Street.

That summer we had our first look at Madison and our first contact with the University of Wisconsin's Mathematics Department. R H Bing was running a one-month Topology conference to which he invited Ellen. I just went along as a husband, but I also participated in one of the seminars. Pop and Irene kept Catherine during that month. We stayed in Kronshage Hall, right on the shore of Lake Mendota, which was very nice because it was miserably hot and the only way to cool off was to jump in the lake. One day, when Ellen did just that, her wedding ring slipped off and was lost in the mud. She was quite visibly pregnant again, which made it fun to go to a jeweler on State Street and announce that we needed a wedding ring.

The estimated time of arrival of our second child was about Nov. 20. About that time Ellen thought that things were about to happen, I took her to the hospital, Mama came up from New York to help take care of Catherine, and then it turned out to be a false alarm. Ellen came back home, and we waited and waited. Mama got tired of it after a few days and also went home.

On Nov. 29, 1955, I became a citizen. Some time in December, the gynecologist took me aside and confessed "You know, with biological processes, you never can tell!"

Finally, on Dec. 29, 1955, Eleanor arrived, after the doctor had decided to induce birth. Someone must have miscalculated pretty badly, because she still looked a bit underdone, and Ellen had no milk for breastfeeding. The doctor suggested the traditional remedy, beer, but the hospital absolutely refused to handle such disreputable stuff. So I bought a couple of six-packs and we had a fine New Years Eve party right there. Next day there was milk, and Eleanor soon lost her underdone look.

Next summer I spent two very pleasant and educational months at the University of Chicago. The main attraction was that Zygmund had persuaded Littlewood to come and give a series of lectures. In addition, Calderon was there, Salem and Helson came, and there were some excellent students around: Eli Stein, Guido and Mary Weiss, Paul Cohen. I was there by myself for the first month, then Ellen joined me after leaving the girls in Houston.

At about that time Papa was found to have Parkinson's disease. Even now there is no cure for this, but there are drugs that control the symptoms – loss of muscle control and loss of memory. In 1956 there was nothing that could help him. He had to stop working and spent most of the summer of 1957 with us in Rochester while Mama held on to her job at Macy's. I think he enjoyed his grandchildren but he got steadily worse.

The last time I saw him fully conscious was when I drove him back to New York before the start of the fall semester. Toward the end of September he suddenly developed a high fever (it was a few days after a urological examination; cause and effect?) and an infection that he was too weak to shake off, even with the help of antibiotics. He was in a coma for almost six weeks until he died, at home, on Nov. 10, 1957. He was only 66. The last words that I heard him say, during a moment when he was semiconscious, were "Don't let them experiment on me!"

(Mama stayed in that same apartment for another 26 years, till she died on May 27, 1983.)

Academic politics began to make life unpleasant in 1956/57. Marshak, chairman of the U. of R. Physics Department which had a very high reputation, and Noyes, a Chemist who, I believe, was Dean of the Graduate School, wanted to see the Mathematics Department raised to the same level. An eminently laudable objective, but the way they went about it was nasty. They looked down their noses at Randolph who, admittedly, produced no research, and took it upon themselves to take over the recruiting for the Mathematics Department, with me as their principal consultant. Several high-salary offers were made to outstanding people. None accepted. We did hire some very good fresh Ph.D.'s, Paul Cohen and Bill Browder among them, but they didn't stay long.

While all this was going on, Washington University tried me again, with an offer of a full professorship. This was immediately matched, since the U. of R. obviously couldn't let me go in the midst of their upgrading campaign, and I stayed. I had arranged to be on leave at Yale during 1958/59, and when Marshak and Noyes kept insisting that everything would be much better if I were in Randolph's place, I gave in and agreed to become chairman on my return. I shouldn't have done that, but I did.

Randolph remained admirably even-tempered throughout all this commotion.

Let's turn to something more pleasant. The next International Congress of Mathematicians (which meets every four years) was to be held in Edinburgh in August 1958. I was a U.S. citizen, I had a beautiful brand-new passport, Ellen had never been to Europe, so we decided to go. Europe was far away then, people hadn't yet got in the habit of just hopping across the Atlantic and back, so to make it worthwhile we planned a 3-month trip. Pop and Irene agreed to keep Catherine and Eleanor for that whole summer! (I did say that she was a fabulous grandmother, didn't I?)

We started with 8 days of pure luxury on the Cristoforo Colombo, an Italian liner that took us from New York to Naples. My only complaint was that the ocean was as smooth as glass. I had been bragging how rough the sea can be, even for large ships, and it just wouldn't show off. Actually it was of course much nicer that way.

In Naples we picked up a Citroen 2 CV, a car with zero acceleration which however reached positive speed (and was thus a counter-example to the fundamental theorem of calculus). But it was a nice little car in which we crisscrossed Italy for a month, then continued into France, where Avignon was one of our first stops. It was not easy to find the Jewish cemetery, and it was even harder to find the man who had the key to the gate, but we did get in and I took some pictures of the graves of Apapa and Amama – something that Mama had particularly wanted me to do.

Next came a week in Montpellier, where Jean-Pierre Kahane had arranged a small totally informal conference which included Mandelbrojt (my mathematical grandfather), Salem, Helson, and Katznelson who was still a student. It was the most civilized conference I have every been to. There was one lecture each morning, followed by a long leisurely lunch, after which we either went to a nearby beach, or to the Roman aquaduct at Nimes, or to some other interesting place for the rest of the day. And by the end of the week a major problem was solved:

In the thirties, Wiener and Paul Lévy had proved that if g is an analytic function and f has an absolutely convergent Fourier series, then so does the composition $g(f)$. The problem was: Are the analytic functions the only ones with this property? Kahane and I had been getting partial results over the last couple of years, leapfrogging each other toward an affirmative answer. Kahane had come closest. It remained to be proved that certain nonlinear transformations satisfied a boundedness condition, and we didn't see how to do that. At one point I heard Helson say to Katznelson "why not try the Baire category theorem?" It seems absurd that that sort of remark could have been the trigger, but, in fact, a clever way of applying that (very standard) theorem enabled Katznelson to finish the job.

A few days later, after we had dispersed, Helson and Kahane did the same thing for Fourier transforms. At the Edinburgh Congress Kahane and I got an even stronger conclusion for Fourier-Stieltjes transforms. And after the dust had settled we extended all this to the setting of locally compact abelian groups in a paper which for several years was referred to as "the four-author paper".

From Montpellier we went to Paris where we spent a week and turned the car in a day earlier than we had to (I felt threatened by the Paris drivers). Then came a nice visit with the Chestertons in Hove, a week in London, and after a few more stops we finally reached Edinburgh. It was quite exciting to meet a lot of people who had only been names so far, especially the few Russians who had been allowed to come.

After the Congress we flew from Glasgow to Boston (on a slow propeller plane), because the AMS summer meeting was at M.I.T. this time and I had been invited to give an hour lecture. The timing couldn't have been better: I could tell them all about the brand-new converse of the Wiener-Lévy theorem.

I had visited Yale during the preceding spring vacation and had rented us a very elegant house in Hamden (for a very cheap price – the owner was an absent-minded professor). We had a very nice year there. The people I was most interested in were Kakutani, Hille, and Rickart.

Sometime that fall I was sitting in my office, minding my own business, when the phone rang. It was R H Bing, who was then chairman, asking me to teach a course in Madison next summer. I was taken by surprise, said something like "I don't really want to teach summer school, I have a Sloan Fellowship, I don't need the money,..." and then my brain slipped out of gear but my tongue kept on talking and I heard it say "but how about a real job?" My subconscious obviously didn't want to go back to Rochester.

A couple of weeks later I was in Madison, being interviewed by Dean Ingraham, a mathematician, and by President Elvejhem, a member of a now extinct species: A president of a major University who spent his afternoons in his Chemistry lab.

Bing called again on Eleanor's birthday: I had my real job.

Epilogue

Madison turned out to be exactly the right kind of place for us – the right kind of city and the right kind of Mathematics Department. There is no point in describing in detail what we did for the next 33 years. I taught my classes, had graduate students, worked with colleagues, wrote papers and books, exactly what a professor is supposed to do. Ellen did the same, first as a part-time temporary lecturer, until she was suddenly promoted to a full professorship in 1970 (the anti-nepotism rules, which were actually never a law, had fallen into disrepute). And both of us lectured here, there, and yonder. (This could now easily degenerate into a travelogue, but I will restrain myself.)

This story began with my ancestors. I will now conclude it with a few words about my offsprings.

Catherine, born in Rochester on July 17, 1954, developed an early interest in folk-dancing (especially in the Balkan varieties) and in languages. This led to her studying Bulgarian as a Freshman at the University of Wisconsin, to a few summers spent at a language institute in Sofia, and finally to a Ph.D. in Linguistics at Indiana University. Her thesis deals with some aspects of Bulgarian syntax. At Indiana she met Ali Eminov, a Ph.D. student in Anthropology. His ancestors had moved from Turkey into Bulgaria a few hundred years ago, had always lived in Turkish villages, and had remained Turks. He ran away to Greece as a teenager, spent a couple of years there in a refugee camp, until a church group brought him to Connecticut.

Catherine and Ali were married in our living room on Dec. 27, 1979. They are both professors at Wayne State University, a small college in Wayne, Nebraska. She is now studying and recording Omaha, an about-to-vanish Indian language that is still spoken by old people on a nearby reservation.

They have two sons, Adem Eminoglu Rudin, born Aug. 2, 1987, and Deniz Erik Rudin, born April 14, 1989, both in Wayne. (Eminoglu is the Turkish name whose Bulgarianized version is Eminov. Ali dislikes the latter.)

Eleanor, born in Rochester on Dec. 29, 1955, was quite precocious; as soon as Catherine learned anything, Eleanor learned it from Catherine. When she was 13 she went with a bus load of Madison kids to work for a month on Black farms in Mississippi. After she got a B.A. in Physics at the University of Wisconsin she moved to St. Paul, Minnesota, and found a position in a small company which designed and manufactured instruments that measure particle sizes (mainly for pollution control devices). She enjoyed this work but felt, after a few years of it, that she ought to know more about Engineering, and enrolled in the University of Minnesota Engineering School. There she got a Master's Degree and met her future husband, Scott Gaff, a descendant of a long line of Minnesotans and a fellow student. They were married in Scott's mother's living room, on Oct. 2, 1982. They live in St. Paul, Scott is an enthusiastic member of a small company that specializes in TV animation, Eleanor is an engineer at 3M. Like Papa, she likes hands-on engineering. She much prefers that to supervising others.

Robert Jefferson, our third child, was born in Madison on May 6, 1961, with Down's syndrome. Needless to say, that was a sad blow. He had major surgery on the first day of his life, to connect his stomach to his intestines. By this time, Lila Hilgendorf, a natural-born mother and helper, had done a lot of baby-sitting and some housecleaning for us. She took Bobbie on as her special project, took him home every weekend, and eventually became his official foster mother until she died in 1985. He now shares an apartment with another retarded man, in a supervised living arrangement, works in two fast food places, and is very involved in Special Olympics. He has far surpassed our early expectations.

Last, but not least, Charles Michael was born in Madison on Feb. 24, 1964. As a teenager, Charlie was a gymnast and diver and played the flute well enough to win several prizes, including a four-year scholarship to the University of Wisconsin, where he enrolled in the medical scholars program, majoring in Biochemistry. In 1986 he was admitted into the University of Chicago's M.D.-Ph.D. program. He has a Biochemistry Ph.D. and an M.D. degree and works as an oncologist at the University of Chicago.

Unlike his sisters who met their future husbands in graduate school, Charlie had Elizabeth Rodini as his girl friend since they were 13, but they waited till Sep. 14, 1991 to get married. Following the family tradition, this took place in our living room. Elizabeth has an Art

History Ph.D., also from the University of Chicago. Their daughter, Sofia Morgan Rudin, was born on June 25, 1995.

Catherine, Eleanor, and Elizabeth have all kept their maiden names.

Ellen and I retired in May 1991. In our case this simply means that we don't teach anymore, but otherwise our life style has hardly changed at all. Mathematicians have a tremendous advantage in this respect over almost everyone else: being retired does not mean that we have to stop doing what we enjoyed over the last 45 years. We can still think about interesting problems, we can still talk about them with colleagues, we can still publish our results, we still get invited to give lectures. And we can spend a month or more each winter on one of our favorite beaches in Hawaii.

How long this will last nobody knows. But I do know that I have had more than my share of life's goodies, and I appreciate it.

Map and Photographs

Map of France

Opapa at 80

Omama

Apapa

Amama

PAPA

in World War II

circa 1930

October 1945

Mama, 1929

Mama, 1954

Betti, Elda, Mama, early 1950s

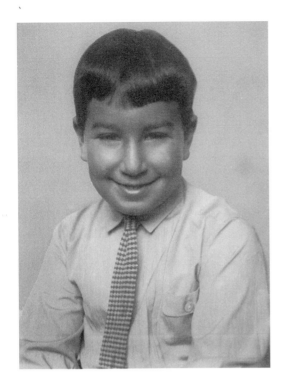

Walter, circa 1930

Vera, circa 1930

Vera, circa 1943

The "Baron Nairn" on June 25, 1940

248 Company Pioneer Corps

with Vera, October 1945

John Gergen, June 1949

Walter at M.I.T.

Raphael Salem, November 1951

Honeymoon, August 1953

Pop

Irene

Catherine, Bobbie, Ellen,
Eleanor, and Charlie
November 1966

Part II

CHAPTER 21

Interchanging Limit Processes

As I mentioned earlier, my thesis (Trans. AMS 68, 1950, 278-303) dealt with uniqueness questions for series of spherical harmonics, also known as Laplace series. In the more familiar setting of trigonometric series, the first theorem of the kind that I was looking for was proved by Georg Cantor in 1870, based on earlier work of Riemann (1854, published in 1867). Using the notations

$$A_n(x) = a_n \cos nx + b_n \sin nx, \quad s_p(x) = A_0 + A_1(x) + \cdots + A_p(x),$$

where a_n and b_n are real numbers, Cantor's theorem says:

If $\lim_{p \to \infty} s_p(x) = 0$ *at every real x, then $a_n = b_n = 0$ for every n.*

Therefore two distinct trigonometric series cannot converge to the same sum. This is what is meant by uniqueness.

My aim was to prove this for spherical harmonics and (as had been done for trigonometric series) to whittle away at the hypotheses. Instead of assuming convergence at every point of the sphere, what sort of summability will do? Does one really need convergence (or summability) at *every* point? If not, what sort of sets can be omitted? Must anything else be assumed at these omitted points? What sort of side conditions, if any, are relevant?

I came up with reasonable answers to these questions, but basically the whole point seemed to be the justification of the interchange of some limit processes. This left me with an uneasy feeling that there ought to be more to Analysis than that. I wanted to do something with more "structure". I could not have explained just what I meant by this, but I found it later when I became aware of the close relation between Fourier analysis and group theory, and also in an occasional encounter with number theory and with geometric aspects of several complex variables.

Why was it all an exercise on interchanging limits? Because the "obvious" proof of Cantor's theorem goes like this: For $p > n$,

$$\pi a_n = \int_{-\pi}^{\pi} s_p(x) \cos nx\, dx = \lim_{p \to \infty} \int_{-\pi}^{\pi} s_p(x) \cos nx\, dx$$

$$= \int_{-\pi}^{\pi} (\lim_{p \to \infty} s_p(x)) \cos nx\, dx$$

$$= \int_{-\pi}^{\pi} 0 \cdot \cos nx\, dx = 0,$$

and similarly for b_n. Note that $\lim \int = \int \lim$ was used.

In Riemann's above-mentioned paper, he derives the conclusion of Cantor's theorem under an additional hypothesis, namely, $a_n \to 0$ and $b_n \to 0$ as $n \to \infty$. He associates to $\sum A_n(x)$ the twice integrated series

$$F(x) = -\sum_{1}^{\infty} n^{-2} A_n(x)$$

and then finds it necessary to prove, in some detail, that this series converges and that its sum F is continuous! (Weierstrass had not yet invented uniform convergence.) This is astonishingly different from most of his other publications, such as his paper on hypergeometric functions in which mind-boggling relations and transformations are merely stated, with only a few hints, or his painfully brief paper on the zeta-function.

In Crelle's J. 72, 1870, 130-138, Cantor showed that Riemann's additional hypothesis was redundant, by proving that

$$(*) \qquad \lim_{n \to \infty} A_n(x) = 0 \quad \text{for all } x \quad \text{implies} \quad \lim_{n \to \infty} a_n = \lim_{n \to \infty} b_n = 0.$$

He included the statement: This cannot be proved, as is commonly believed, by term-by-term integration.

Apparently it took a while before this was generally understood. Ten years later, in Math. Annalen 16, 1880, 113-114, he patiently explains the difference between pointwise convergence and uniform convergence, in order to refute a "simpler proof" published by Appell. But then, referring to his second (still quite complicated) proof, the one in Math. Annalen 4, 1871, 139-143, he sticks his neck out and writes: "In my opinion, no further simplification can be achieved, given the nature of the subject."

That was a bit reckless. 25 years later, Lebesgue's dominated convergence theorem became part of every analyst's tool chest, and since then $(*)$ can be proved in a few lines:

Rewrite $A_n(x)$ in the form $A_n(x) = c_n \cos(nx + \alpha_n)$, where $c_n^2 = a_n^2 + b_n^2$. Put

$$\gamma_n = \min\{1, |c_n|\}, \quad B_n(x) = \gamma_n \cos(nx + \alpha_n).$$

Then $B_n^2(x) \leq 1, B_n^2(x) \to 0$ at every x, so that the D. C. Th., combined with

$$\int_{-\pi}^{\pi} B_n^2(x)dx = \pi\gamma_n^2$$

shows that $\gamma_n \to 0$. Therefore $|c_n| = \gamma_n$ for all large n, and $c_n \to 0$. Done.

The point of all this is that my attitude was probably wrong. Interchanging limit processes occupied some of the best mathematicians for most of the 19th century. Thomas Hawkins' book "Lebesgue's Theory" gives an excellent description of the difficulties that they had to overcome. Perhaps we should not be too surprised that even a hundred years later many students are baffled by uniform convergence, uniform continuity, etc., and that some never get it at all.

In Trans. AMS 70, 1951, 387-403, I applied the techniques of my thesis to another problem of this type, with Hermite functions in place of spherical harmonics.

CHAPTER 22

Function Algebras

When I arrived at M.I.T. in 1950, Banach algebras were one of the hot topics. Gelfand's 1941 paper "Normierte Ringe" had apparently only reached the U.S. in the late forties, and circulated on hard-to-read smudged purple ditto copies. As one application of the general theory presented there, it contained a stunningly short proof of Wiener's lemma: the Fourier series of the reciprocal of a nowhere vanishing function with absolutely convergent Fourier series also converges absolutely. Not only was the proof extremely short, it was one of those that are hard to forget. All one needs to remember is that the absolutely convergent Fourier series form a Banach algebra, and that every multiplicative linear functional on this algebra is evaluation at some point of the unit circle.

This may have led some to believe that Banach algebras would now solve all our problems. Of course they couldn't, but they did provide the right framework for many questions in analysis (as does most of functional analysis) and, conversely, abstract questions about Banach algebras often gave rise to interesting problems in hard analysis. ("Hard" is used here as Hardy and Littlewood used it. For example, you do "hard analysis" when, in order to estimate some integral, you break it into three pieces and apply different inequalities to each.)

One type of Banach algebras that was soon studied in detail were the so-called function algebras, also known as uniform algebras.

To see what these are, let $C(X)$ be the set of all *complex-valued* continuous functions on a compact Hausdorff space X. A *function algebra on X* is a subset A of $C(X)$ such that

(i) if f and g are in A, so are $f+g$, fg, and cf for every complex number c (this says that A is an algebra),

(ii) A contains the constant functions,

(iii) A separates points on X (i.e., if $p \neq q$, both in X, then $f(p) \neq f(q)$ for some f in A), and

(iv) A is closed, relative to the sup-norm topology of $C(X)$, i.e., the topology in which convergence means uniform convergence.

A is said to be *self-adjoint* if the complex conjugate of every f in A is also in A. The most familiar example of a non-self-adjoint function algebra is the *disc algebra* $A(U)$ which consists of all f in $C(\overline{U})$ that are holomorphic in U. (Here, and later, U is the open unit disc in $\mathbb{C}$, the complex plane, and $\overline{U}$ is its closure.) I have already described my first encounter with $A(U)$ in Chapter 19, a propos maximum modulus algebras.

One type of question that was asked over and over again was: Suppose that a function algebra on X satisfies $\cdots$ and $\cdots$ and $\cdots$. Is it $C(X)$? (In fact, 20 years later a whole book, entitled "Characterizations of $C(X)$ among its Subalgebras" was published by R. B. Burckel.) The Stone-Weierstrass Theorem gives the classical answer: Yes, if A is self-adjoint.

There are problems even when X is a compact interval I on the real line. For instance, suppose A is a function algebra on I, and to every maximal ideal M of A corresponds a point p in I such that M is the set of all f in A having $f(p) = 0$. (In other words, the only maximal ideals of A are the obvious ones.) Is $A = C(I)$? This is still unknown, in 1995.

If $f_1, \cdots, f_n$ are in $C(I)$, and the n-tuple $(f_1, \cdots, f_n)$ separates points on I, let $A(f_1, \cdots, f_n)$ be the smallest closed subalgebra of $C(I)$ that contains $f_1, \cdots f_n$ and 1.

When f_1 is one-to-one on I, it follows from an old theorem of Walsh (Math. Annalen 96, 1926, 437-450) that $A(f_1) = C(I)$.

Stone-Weierstrass implies that $A(f_1, \cdots, f_n) = C(I)$ if each f_i is real-valued.

In the other direction, John Wermer showed, in Annals of Math. 62, 1955, 267-270, that $A(f_1, f_2, f_3)$ can be a *proper* subset of $C(I)$!

Here is how he did this:

Let E be an arc in $\mathbb{C}$, of positive two-dimensional measure, and let A_E be the algebra of all continuous functions on the Riemann sphere S (the one-point compactification of $\mathbb{C}$) which are holomorphic in the complement of E. He showed that $g(E) = g(S)$ for every g in A_E, that A_E contains a triple (g_1, g_2, g_3) that separates points on S, and that the restriction of A_E to E is closed in $C(E)$. Pick a homeomorhism φ of I onto E and define $f_i = g_i \circ \varphi$. Then $A(f_1, f_2, f_3) \neq C(I)$, for if h is in $A(f_1, f_2, f_3)$ then $h = g \circ \varphi$ for some g in A_E, so that

$$h(I) = g(E) = g(S)$$

is the closure of an open subset of $\mathbb{C}$ (except when h is constant).

In order to prove the same with two function instead of three I replaced John's arc E with a Cantor set K, also of positive two-dimensional measure. (I use the term "Cantor set" for any totally disconnected compact metric space with no isolated points; these are all homeomorphic to each other.) A small extra twist, applied to John's argument, with A_K in place of A_E, proved that $A(f_1, f_2)$ can also be smaller than $C(I)$.

I also used A_K to show that $C(K)$ contains maximal closed point-separating subalgebras that are not maximal ideals, and that the same is true for $C(X)$ whenever X contains a Cantor set. These ideas were pushed further by Hoffman and Singer in Acta Math. 103, 1960, 217-241.

In the same paper I showed that $A(f_1, \cdots, f_n) = C(I)$ when $n - 1$ of the n given functions are real-valued.

Since Wermer's paper was being published in the Annals, and mine strengthened his theorem and contained other interesting (at least to me) results, I sent mine there too. It was rejected, almost by return mail, by an anonymous editor, for not being sufficiently interesting. I have had a few other papers rejected over the years, but for better reasons. This one was published in Proc. AMS 7, 1956, 825-830, and is one of six whose Russian translations were made into a book "Some Questions in Approximation Theory"; the others were three by Bishop and two by Wermer. Good company.

Later, Gabriel Stolzenberg (Acta Math. 115, 1966, 185-198) and Herbert Alexander (Amer. J. Math. 93, 1971, 65-74) went much more deeply into these problems. One of the highlights in Alexander's paper is:

$A(f_1, \cdots, f_n) = C(I)$ if $f_1, \cdots, f_{n-1}$ are of bounded variation.

A propos the Annals (published by Princeton University) here is a little Princeton anecdote. During a week that I spent there, in the mid-eighties, the Institute threw a cocktail party. (What I enjoyed best at that affair was being attacked by Armand Borel for having said, in print, that sheaves had vanished into the background.) Next morning I overheard the following conversation in Fine Hall:

Prof. A. That was a nice party yesterday, wasn't it?

Prof. B. Yes, and wasn't it nice that they invited the whole department?

Prof. A. Well, only the full professors.

Prof. B. Of course.

The above-mentioned facts about Cantor sets led me to look at the opposite extreme, the so-called scattered spaces. A compact Hausdorff space Q is said to be scattered if Q contains no perfect set; every nonempty compact set F in Q thus contains a point that is not a limit point of F. The principal result proved in Proc. AMS 8, 1957, 39-42 is:

THEOREM. *Every closed subalgebra of $C(Q)$ is self-adjoint.*

In fact, the scattered spaces are the only ones for which this is true, but I did not state this in that paper.

In 1956 I found a very explicit description of all closed ideals in the disc algebra $A(U)$ (defined at the beginning of this chapter). The description involves *inner function.* These are the bounded holomorphic functions in U whose radial limits have absolute value 1 at almost every point of the unit circle $\mathbb{T}$. They play a very important role in the study of holomorphic functions in U (see, for instance, Garnett's book *Bounded Analytic Functions*), and their analogues will be mentioned again, on Riemann surfaces, in polydiscs, and in balls in $\mathbb{C}^n$.

Recall that a point ζ on $\mathbb{T}$ is called a *singular point* of a holomorphic function f in U if f has no analytic continuation to any neighborhood of ζ. The ideals in question are described by the following

THEOREM. *Let E be a compact subset of $\mathbb{T}$, of Lebesgue measure 0, let u be an inner function all of whose singular points lie in E, and let $J(E,u)$ be the set of all f in $A(U)$ such that*
    (i) *the quotient f/u is bounded in U, and*
    (ii) *$f(\zeta) = 0$ at every ζ in E.*
Then $J(E,u)$ is a closed ideal of $A(U)$, and every closed ideal of $A(U)(\neq \{0\})$ is obtained in this way.

One of several corollaries is that every closed ideal of $A(U)$ is principal, i.e., is generated by a single function.

I presented this at the December 1956 AMS meeting in Rochester, and was immediately told by several people that Beurling had proved the same thing, in a course he had given at Harvard, but had not published it. I was also told that Beurling might be quite upset at this, and that having Beurling upset at you was not a good thing. Having used his famous paper about the shift operator on a Hilbert space as my guide, I was not surprised that he too had proved this, but I saw no reason to withdraw my already submitted paper. It appeared in Canadian J. Math. 9, 1957, 426-434. The result is now known as the Beurling-Rudin theorem. I met him several times later, and he never made a fuss over this.

In the preceding year Lennart Carleson and I, neither of us knowing what the other was doing, proved what is now known as the Rudin-Carleson interpolation theorem. His paper is in Math. Z. 66, 1957, 447-451, mine in Proc. AMS 7, 1956, 808-811:

THEOREM. *If E is a compact subset of $\mathbb{T}$, of Lebesgue measure 0, then every f in $C(E)$ extends to a function F in $A(U)$.*

(It is easy to see that this fails if $m(E) > 0$. To say that F is an extension of f means simply that $F(\zeta) = f(\zeta)$ at every ζ in E.)

Our proofs have some ingredients in common, but they are different, and we each proved more than is stated above. Surprisingly, Carleson, the master of classical hard analysis, used a soft approach, namely duality in Banach spaces, and concluded that F could be so chosen that $\|F\|_U \le 2\|f\|_E$. (The norms are sup-norms over the sets appearing as subscripts.) In the same paper he used his Banach space argument to prove another interpolation theorem, involving Fourier-Stieltjes transforms.

On the other hand, I did not have functional analysis in mind at all, I did not think of norms or of Banach spaces, I proved, by a bare-hands construction combined with the Riemann mapping theorem that if Ω is a closed Jordan domain containing $f(E)$ then F can be so chosen that $F(\overline{U})$ also lies in Ω. If Ω is a disc, centered at 0, this gives $\|F\|_U = \|f\|_E$, so F is a norm-preserving extension.

What our proofs had in common is that we both used part of the construction that was used in the original proof of the F. and M. Riesz theorem (which says that if a measure μ on $\mathbb{T}$ gives $\int f d\mu = 0$ for every f in $A(U)$ then μ is absolutely continuous with respect to Lebesgue measure). Carleson showed, in fact, that F. and M. Riesz can be derived quite easily from the interpolation theorem. I tried to prove the implication in the other direction. But that had to wait for Errett Bishop. In Proc. AMS 13, 1962, 140-143, he established this implication in a very general setting which had nothing to do with holomorphic functions or even with algebras, and which, combined with a refinement due to Glicksberg (Trans. AMS 105, 1962, 415-435) makes the interpolation theorem even more precise:

THEOREM. *One can choose F in $A(U)$ so that $F(\zeta) = f(\zeta)$ at every ζ in E, and $|f(z)| < \|f\|_E$ at every z in $\overline{U}\backslash E$.*

This is usually called peak-interpolation.

Several variable analogues of this and related results may be found in Chap. 6 of my *Function Theory in Polydiscs* and in Chap. 10 of my *Function Theory in the Unit Ball of $\mathbb{C}^n$*.

The last item in this chapter concerns Riemann surfaces. Some definitions are needed.

A *finite Riemann surface* is a connected open proper subset R of some compact Riemann surface X, such that the boundary ∂R of R in X is also the boundary of its closure $\overline{R}$ and is the union of finitely many disjoint simple closed analytic curves $\Gamma_1, \cdots \Gamma_k$. Shrinking each Γ_i to a point gives a compact orientable manifold whose genus g is defined to be the genus of R. The numbers g and k determine the topology of R, but not, of course, its conformal structure.

$A(R)$ denotes the algebra of all continuous functions on $\overline{R}$ that are holomorphic in R. If f is in $A(R)$ and $|f(p)| = 1$ at every point p in ∂R then, just as in U, f is called *inner*. A set $S \subset A(R)$ is *unramified* if every point of $\overline{R}$ has a neighborhood in which at least one member of S is one-to-one.

I became interested in these algebras when Lee Stout (Math. Z. 92, 1966, 366-379; also 95, 1967, 403-404) showed that every $A(R)$ contains an unramified triple of inner functions that separates points on $\overline{R}$. He deduced from the resulting embedding of R in U^3 that $A(R)$ is generated by these 3 functions. Whether every $A(R)$ is generated by some pair of its member of still unknown, but the main result of my paper in Trans. AMS 150, 1969, 423-434 shows that pairs of inner functions won't always do:

THEOREM. *If $A(R)$ contains a point-separating unramified pair f, g of inner functions, then there exist relatively prime integers s and t such that f is s - to - 1 and g is t - to - 1 on every Γ_i, and*

$$(*) \qquad\qquad (ks - 1)(kt - 1) = 2g + k - 1.$$

For example, when $g = 2$ and $k = 4$, then $(*)$ holds for no integers s and t. When $g = 23$ and $k = 4$, then $s = t = 2$ is the only pair that satisfies $(*)$, but it it not relatively prime. Even when $R = U$ the theorem gives some information. In that case $g = 0, k = 1$, so $(*)$ becomes $(s - 1)(t - 1) = 0$, which means:

If a pair of finite Blaschke products separates points on $\overline{U}$ and their derivatives have no common zero in U, then at least one of them is one-to-one (i.e., is a Moebius transformation).

There are two cases in which (∗) is not only necessary but also sufficient. This happens when $g = 0$ and when $g = k = 1$.

But there are examples in which the topological condition (∗) is satisfied even though the conformal structure of R prevents the existence of a separating unramified pair of inner functions.

This paper is quite different from anything else that I have ever done. As far as I know, no one has ever referred to it, but I had fun working on it.

CHAPTER 23

Misteaks

Mathematicians are human. Humans make mistakes. Therefore $\cdots$.

This is no cause for alarm. I have no figures to back this up, but compared to the flood of published papers, the number of serious errors in the literature must be tiny. Most are probably caught by referees. And if there is a serious error in a paper that is important enough to be studied by a significant number of interested mathematicians, that error will be discovered. Even better, the one who made it won't be able to argue his way out of it.

There is an amusing article by Geoffrey K. Pullum in Natural Language and Linguistic Theory 5, 1987, 303-309, which compares this social aspect of mathematics with what happens in linguistics. It describes the story of Rourke's claim to have proved the Poincaré conjecture. (The article was sent to me by Catherine, my linguist daughter.)

My first encounter with this sort of thing started with the letter on the following page.

Needless to say, I was totally amazed. Here was Dieudonné, a world-class mathematician and one of the founders of Bourbaki, not telling me, a young upstart, "you are wrong, because here is what I proved a few years ago" but asking me, instead, to tell him what he had done wrong! Actually, it took me a while to find the error, and if I had not proved earlier (in J. Math. Mech. 7, 1958, 103-116) that convolution-factorization is always possible in L^1 I would have accepted his conclusion with no hesitation, not because he was famous, but because his argument was simple and perfectly correct, *as far as it went*.

He proved, correctly, that every convolution of nonnegative functions coincides almost everywhere with one that is lower semicontinuous. But (and this is what he ignored) *that function may have $+\infty$ among its values*.

NORTHWESTERN UNIVERSITY

EVANSTON, ILLINOIS

58, Rue de Verneuil, Paris 7e (France)

Paris, December 17

Dear Professor Rudin:

In the last issue of the Bulletin AMS, I see that you announce in abstract 731t, p.382, that in the algebra $L^1(R^n)$, any element is the convolution of two elements of that algebra. I am rather amazed at that statement, for a few years ago I had made a simple remark which seemed to me to disprove your theorem (Compositio Mathematica, 12 (1954) p.17, footnote 3). I reproduce the proof for your convenience:

Suppose f, g are in L^1 and ≥ 0, and for each n consider the usual "truncated" functions $f_n = \inf(f, n)$ and $g_n = \inf(g, n)$; f (resp. g) is the limit of the increasing sequence (f_n) (resp. (g_n)), hence, by the usual Lebesgue convergence theorem, $h = f * g$ is a.e. the limit of $h_n = f_n * g_n$, which is obviously an increasing sequence. Moreover, f_n and g_n are both in L^2, hence it is well known that h_n can be taken <u>continuous</u> and bounded. It follows that h is a.e. equal to a Baire function of the <u>first class</u>. However, it is well known that there are integrable functions which <u>do not</u> have that property, and therefore they cannot be convolutions.

I am unable to find any flaw in that argument, and if you can do so, I would very much appreciate if you can tell me where I am wrong.

Sincerely yours

J. Dieudonné

His argument proves that there are nonnegative functions h in L^1 that are not representable as $h = f * g$ with $f \geq 0$ and $g \geq 0$. (I had also observed this.) In the general (real-valued) case, if $h = f * g$, each of f and g is a difference of two nonnegative functions, so that $f * g$ breaks into four convolutions of the type considered by Dieudonné. Of these, two are ≥ 0, two are ≤ 0, and one may therefore run into the problem of subtracting ∞ from ∞ (which is at least as much of a no-no as is dividing 0 by 0). Hence one can no longer conclude that h coincides almost everywhere with a function of Baire class one, i.e., with a *real-valued* function which is *everywhere* the pointwise limit of a sequence of continuous ones.

Dieudonné had fallen into the "without loss of generality" trap by restricting himself to $f \geq 0$ and $g \geq 0$, and by tacitly assuming that the general case would follow.

Here is his reply to my explanation.

Paris, January 12, 1958

Dear Professor Rudin:

Thank you for pointing out my error; as it is of a very common type, I suppose I should have been able to detect it myself, but you know how hard it is to see one's own mistakes, when you have once become convinced that some result must be true!!

Your proof is very ingenious; I hope you will be able to generalize that result to arbitrary locally compact abelian groups, but I suppose this would require a somewhat different type of proof.

With my congratulations for your nice result and my best thanks, I am

Sincerely yours

J. Dieudonné

The factorization theorem was indeed extended, even further than he had hoped. When Paul Cohen saw my rather complicated proof about $L^1(\mathbb{R}^n)$ (the case $n = 1$ was much easier) he said "Aha, approximate identities" and quickly produced a very general factorization theorem in Banach algebras with approximate left identities (Duke Math. J. 26, 1959, 199-205). Ed Hewitt (Math. Scand. 15, 1964, 147-155) extended Cohen's proof so as to include convolution operators on $L^p (1 \leq p < \infty)$: Every h in L^p is $f * g$ with f in L^1, g in L^p.

In my next story, I was the one who goofed, but it ended well. This concerned the open unit ball B in the n-dimensional complex space $\mathbb{C}^n$. A one-to-one holomorphic map from B onto B will be called an *automorphism* of B. (When $n = 1$, B is the unit disc in $\mathbb{C}$, and its automorphisms are the familiar Moebius transformations that send z to $e^{i\theta}(z - \alpha)/(1 - \overline{\alpha}z)$. The automorphisms of B are also explicitly known for all n. They will be described in Chapter 30.)

Call a space X of complex-valued functions on B (or on the boundary of B) Moebius-invariant (or $\mathcal{M}$-invariant) if the composition $f \circ \varphi$ is in X for every f in X and every automorphism φ of B. Alex Nagel and I had found all $\mathcal{M}$-invariant spaces of certain types (Duke Math. J. 43, 10976, 841-861) but the following was not answered:

Which closed subalgebras of $C(B)$ are $\mathcal{M}$-invariant?

Here $C(B)$ is the algebra of all complex-valued continuous (possibly unbounded) functions on B, with the topology of uniform convergence on compact sets, and with pointwise addition and multiplication.

The five obvious possibilities are: $\{0\}$, the constants, the holomorphic functions on B, those whose complex conjugates are holomorphic, and $C(B)$ itself. The answer (Ann. Inst. Fourier 23, 1983, 19-41) is:

THEOREM. *There are no others.*

I believe that this is the most difficult theorem that I ever proved. It was new even for $n = 1$. I started with a proof of the one-dimensional case, and then used that to derive the same conclusion in n dimensions. Fairly soon after I submitted the paper, Malgrange, who was an editor of Annales Fourier, wrote that the referee did not understand how I passed from 1 to n. When I looked at it, I couldn't understand it either! What I had written simply made no sense, and there seemed to be no way to repair it. I had to go back and instead of first dealing with the one-variable case I had to do the whole thing in n variables from the start. Fortunately, it worked. But it took a whole summer.

When I sent the corrected (much longer) version to Malgrange, I wrote that I would like to thank the referee in the revised paper, but only if I could mention his or her name. I saw no virtue in anonymous thanks. The referee agreed to this: it turned out to be my friend Jean-Pierre Rosay.

A few years later we (i.e., the Madison Mathematics Department) wanted to invite Rosay for a year's visit. I had a so-called Vilas Professorship which provided research funds for worthy projects. So I sent a request to the appropriate committee; to strengthen the case, I mentioned that not only I but several of my colleagues (Ahern, Forelli, Nagel, Wainger among them) would find him very stimulating. My letter was returned by no other than Irv Shain, the Chancellor, saying that this was no good, that Vilas Professorships were only for the benefit of those who had one and for no one else's, and that I should write a different letter, explaining how Rosay's presence would benefit me. I did that, and as a clincher enclosed a reprint of the paper in which I thanked him. That did it.

Soon after he arrived, he and I started to work on several questions about holomorphic maps. This resulted in a long paper (Trans. AMS 310, 1988, 47-86), the first of several that we wrote together. (Some details of this may be found in Chapter 31.) Our collaboration went so well that I suggested that we ought to try to keep him. We succeeded in this, and it could well be that my role in getting him to stay here was one of the best things I ever did for the Department.

I know of only one totally absurd paper that was published in a respectable journal, namely the one by Nikola Pandeski in Math. Annalen 287, 1990, 185-192. In one variable, the "corona theorem" asserts that the open unit disc U is dense in the maximal ideal space of the Banach algebra of all bounded holomorphic functions in U. Its original proof, by Lennart Carleson (Annals of Math. 76, 1962, 547-559) involved a great deal of difficult "hard" analysis. A much simpler one was later found by Tom Wolff (see Chap. VIII in Garnett's *Bounded Analytic Functions*). But the n-variable analogue, which Pandeski claimed to have proved, is still wide open.

This paper appeared during a several complex variables conference in Oberwolfach. I heard that it caused great hilarity because nothing in it makes any sense. For example, the proof starts by covering a sphere with a finite *disjoint* collection of small balls! I have heard several explanations about how this absurdity got into print, none of them convincing. I was quite annoyed about the whole affair because Pandeski attributed

several absolutely false assertions to me, and because Grauert, the editor
who had (mis)handled this paper refused to publish my protest.

CHAPTER 24

$\beta\mathbb{N}$ and CH and All That

As I mentioned earlier, there was a one month topology conference in Madison in 1955 in which I participated as a husband. Homogeneity and compactifications were two frequently heard topics that attracted my attention and which led to the following

QUESTION. If X is homogeneous, is $\beta X \backslash X$ homogeneous?

(Notation: $A \backslash B$ is the set of all members of A that are not in B.) To explain the terminology,

(a) to say that X is *homogeneous* means that X is a topological space in which to every pair of points p and q corresponds a homeomorphism of X onto X that carries p to q, and

(b) if (to be technically correct) X is completely regular then βX is a compact Hausdorff space in which X is dense, and every bounded continuous real-valued function on X extends to a continuous function on βX.

These requirements characterize βX, up to homeomorphisms.

My interest in βX may have been at least partly due to the fact that it is the maximal ideal space of the Banach algebra of all bounded continuous functions on X. When we got back to Rochester I decided to tackle the simplest case of the question: for X I took $\mathbb{N}$, the set of all positive integers, with every singleton an open set.

The original proof of the existence of βX used the bounded continuous functions on X to embed X in a Tychonov cube; the closure of the embedded copy of X is βX. I did not find this very enlightening, nor did the maximal ideals give any help with my problem. But the following set-theoretic description of $\beta\mathbb{N}$ turned out to be exactly what I could use.

Define an *ultrafilter* on $\mathbb{N}$ to be a collection Ω of nonempty subsets of $\mathbb{N}$ such that

(i) if A and B are in Ω, so is their intersection, and

(ii) Ω is maximal with respect to (i).

To every n in $\mathbb{N}$ corresponds a "fixed" Ω_n, consisting of all subsets of $\mathbb{N}$ that contain n. The other Ω's, the interesting ones, are called "free".

Consider now a space Y whose points are the ultrafilters Ω. Associate to each subset A of $\mathbb{N}$ the set V_A of those Ω's that have A as a member, and declare a set in Y to be open if and only if it is a union of V_A's. If Ω_n is identified with n it is not hard to verify that Y has all properties that are required of $\beta\mathbb{N}$, and that therefore Y "is" $\beta\mathbb{N}$.

Let c denote the cardinality of the continuum (which is also the cardinality of the collection of all subsets of $\mathbb{N}$) and let CH stand for "continuum hypothesis" – the statement that c is the smallest uncountable cardinal number.

Using the above description of $\beta\mathbb{N}$ I proved (Duke Math. J. 23, 1956, 409-420), on the basis of CH, that $\beta\mathbb{N}\backslash\mathbb{N}$ has P-points. (These are points x such that every intersection of countably many neighborhoods of x contains a neighborhood of x.) If $\beta\mathbb{N}\backslash\mathbb{N}$ were homogeneous, all of its points would thus be P-points, hence, being compact, $\beta\mathbb{N}\backslash\mathbb{N}$ would be finite. But $\beta\mathbb{N}\backslash\mathbb{N}$ has 2^c points (without CH).

CONCLUSION. CH implies that $\beta\mathbb{N}\backslash\mathbb{N}$ is not homogeneous.

Moreover, still using CH, the P-points form a dense subset of $\beta\mathbb{N}\backslash\mathbb{N}$, there are 2^c of them, and to every pair of them corresponds a homeomorphism of $\beta\mathbb{N}\backslash\mathbb{N}$ onto $\beta\mathbb{N}\backslash\mathbb{N}$ which carries one to the other. (So there is a remnant of homogeneity.)

This paper is the only one in which I have used CH. Frolik (Bull AMS 73, 1967, 87-91) proved later that $\beta\mathbb{N}\backslash\mathbb{N}$ is not homogeneous, without using CH, but the status of P-points remained in doubt for 25 years, until Shelah produced a model of set theory in which $\beta\mathbb{N}\backslash\mathbb{N}$ has none. His proof was written up ty E. L. Wimmers, in Israel J. Math. 43, 1982, 28-48.

In Duke Math. J. 25, 1958, 197-204 I returned to $\beta\mathbb{N}$, in order to answer a question about summability posed by Meyer Jerison. At the end of that paper I asked whether the inhomogeneity of $\beta\mathbb{N}\backslash\mathbb{N}$ was a consequence of the fact that there are no convergent sequences in $\beta\mathbb{N}\backslash\mathbb{N}$. In other words:

Does every homogeneous compact Hausdorff space contain a convergent sequence?

I gave an affirmative answer for compact abelian groups, and have been told by Arkhangelskii that "abelian" can be dropped. The general case seems to be still open.

This was my last contact with βN. The Rudin in the so-called "Rudin-Keisler order" (a partial order on βN) is Ellen.

At this point it is very tempting to preach a short sermon on CH, and I won't resist the temptation.

Every mathematician knows nowadays – at least from hearsay – that neither CH nor its negation can be proved from "the usual axioms of set theory" (which usually means ZFC, Zermelo-Frankel set theory plus the axiom of choice) and that CH is therefore "undecidable". That conclusion upsets me. It conjures up the unappealing vision that humanity will never know.

To try to explain my objection I will compare the status of CH with the role played by the parallel axiom in Euclid's scheme of plane geometry. For 2000 years mathematicians tried to deduce it from his other axioms, until its negation was shown to be also consistent with them. But nevertheless, the axiom is true in the "real" plane. This could of course not be proved before there was a definition, or, better, a description of the "real" plane in terms that had mathematical meaning. Euclid's axioms only list properties of points and lines but don't say what a line *is*. The description of what we regard as the "real" plane had to wait for analytic geometry. "Points" are now ordered pairs of real numbers, the "plane" is the set of all these points, and a "line" is the set of all points (x, y) that satisfy an equation $ax + by + c = 0$, with $a^2 + b^2 > 0$. If $a'x + b'y + c' = 0$ defines another line, it is now a matter of baby algebra to show that they intersect if and only if $ab' \neq a'b$. The parallel axiom follows.

According to the logicians, I am a Platonist (is that good or bad?) because I believe, optimistically, that something similar could happen in set theory. I see no reason why some so far unobserved feature of infinite cardinals could not be discovered which would lead to a more informative description of them, a description which (a) will be so natural that it will be generally accepted (just as "plane = $\mathbb{R} \times \mathbb{R}$" is accepted) and (b) will make it clear, or at least provable, that either CH or its negation is true.

I root for CH.

CHAPTER 25

Idempotent Measures

An idempotent, relative to any multiplication, is simply an element that is its own square. The starting point of my interest in this topic was Henry Helson's complete description (in Proc. AMS 4, 1953, 686-691) of the idempotents in $M(\mathbb{T})$. This is the algebra of all complex Borel measures on the unit circle $\mathbb{T}$ (i.e., on the multiplicative group of the complex numbers of absolute value 1) with convolution as multiplication: if μ and λ are in $M(\mathbb{T})$, their convolution $\mu * \lambda$ is the measure that satisfies

$$\int_{\mathbb{T}} f d(\mu * \lambda) = \int_{\mathbb{T}^2} f(xy) d\mu(x) d\lambda(y)$$

for every f in $C(\mathbb{T})$. The Fourier coefficients of μ,

$$\hat{\mu}(n) = \int_{\mathbb{T}} x^{-n} d\mu(x)$$

therefore satisfy

$$(\mu * \lambda)\hat{\ }(n) = \hat{\mu}(n)\hat{\lambda}(n)$$

for all n in $\mathbb{Z}$, the additive group of the integers. Consequently, each idempotent in $M(\mathbb{T})$, i.e., each μ such that

$$\mu * \mu = \mu$$

has $\hat{\mu}(n) = 0$ or 1 for every n. In other words, $\hat{\mu}$ is the characteristic function of some subset of $\mathbb{Z}$. Helson's theorem tells us what these subsets are:

A function $\alpha : \mathbb{Z} \to \{0,1\}$ is $\hat{\mu}$ for some idempotent μ in $M(\mathbb{T})$ if and only if α differs from a periodic function in at most finitely many places.

The next two theorems I want to quote refer to $A(\mathbb{T})$, the algebra of all functions on $\mathbb{T}$ whose Fourier series converges absolutely, and to $A(\mathbb{R})$, the algebra of all functions on the real line $\mathbb{R}$ that are Fourier transforms of some f in $L^1(\mathbb{R})$. In general, if Ω is some class of functions on a set X, let us say that a function $\varphi : X \to X$ *preserves* Ω if the composition $f \circ \varphi$ is in Ω for every f in Ω.

Beurling and Helson proved: *A function* $\varphi : \mathbb{R} \to \mathbb{R}$ *preserves* $A(\mathbb{R})$ *if and only if* $\varphi(x) = ax + b$ *for some* $a, b, a \neq 0$. *(Math. Scand. 1, 1953, 120-126.)*

Kahane proved: *A function* $\varphi : \mathbb{T} \to \mathbb{T}$ *preserves* $A(\mathbb{T})$ *if and only if* $\varphi(e^{i\theta}) = e^{i(n\theta + b)}$ *for some integer* $n \neq 0$ *and some real number* b. *(C. R. Acad. Sci. Paris, 240, 1955, 36-37.)*

Seeing these two theorems, one is almost forced to ask: What happens when $\mathbb{R}$ and $\mathbb{T}$ are replaced by $\mathbb{Z}$? I found this question fascinating, began to work on it, and found the following beautiful (even if I say so myself) answer. It certainly satisfied my craving for "structure" that I mentioned in connection with my thesis, and it got me hooked on doing Fourier analysis on abelian groups.

By analogy with the preceding definitions, let $A(\mathbb{Z})$ consist of the functions $\hat{f}$ that are Fourier transforms of some f in $L^1(\mathbb{T})$:

$$\hat{f}(n) = \int_T x^{-n} f(x) d\sigma(x)$$

for all n in $\mathbb{Z}$. Here σ is the Haar measure of $\mathbb{T}$, i.e., Lebesgue measure divided by 2π.

THEOREM (Acta Math. 95, 1956, 39-55). *A function* $\varphi : \mathbb{Z} \to \mathbb{Z}$ *preserves* $A(\mathbb{Z})$ *if and only if*

(i) *there is a positive integer* q *and a function* $\psi : \mathbb{Z} \to \mathbb{Z}$ *whose restriction to each residue class (mod* q) *is affine and not constant, and*

(ii) $\varphi(n) = \psi(n)$ *except possibly at finitely many* n.

More explicitly, (i) means that there are integers a_j and non-zero integers b_j such that

$$\psi(j + mq) = a_j + m b_j$$

for $j = 0, 1, \cdots q - 1$ and all m in $\mathbb{Z}$. For example, with $q = 4$ one might have

$$\varphi(4m) = 6m, \varphi(1+4m) = 1+3m, \varphi(2+4m) = 3+6m, \varphi(3+4m) = 2-3m.$$

This φ is even a one-to-one map of $\mathbb{Z}$ onto $\mathbb{Z}$. Hence it induces an automorphism of the convolution algebra $L^1(\mathbb{T})$. Moreover, every automorphism of $L^1(\mathbb{T})$ is obtained in this way, from a permutation φ of $\mathbb{Z}$ that satisfies (i) and (ii).

Helson's theorem played an important role in the proof that (i) and (ii) are necessary.

Every residue class (mod q) is a coset of the subgroup of $\mathbb{Z}$ generated by q, and every singleton is a coset of the subgroup $\{0\}$. This made the group-theoretic nature of the theorem apparent, and suggested that analogues might exist on arbitrary locally compact abelian (LCA) groups G and their duals $\hat{G}$. ($\hat{G}$ is the group of all continuous homomorphisms of G into $\mathbb{T}$. Examples: $\hat{\mathbb{T}} = \mathbb{Z}, \hat{\mathbb{Z}} = \mathbb{T}, \hat{\mathbb{R}} = \mathbb{R}$; here $=$ means "isomorphic to".)

In Pac. J. Math. 9, 1959, 195-209 I defined the *coset-ring* of $\hat{G}$ to be the smallest family of sets that contains all cosets of open subgroups of $\hat{G}$ and is closed under the formation of finite unions, finite intersections, and complementation. Using this terminology, Helson's theorem says that μ is idempotent in $M(\mathbb{T})$ if and only if $\hat{\mu}$ is the characteristic function of some member of the coset-ring of $\mathbb{Z}$. This led to the following

CONJECTURE. *On every LCA group G, a measure μ is idempotent if and only if $\hat{\mu} = 1$ on some member of the coset-ring of $\hat{G}$, and is 0 on the rest of $\hat{G}$.*

I proved this for $G = \mathbb{T}^n$, in which case $\hat{G} = \mathbb{Z}^n$, the group of all lattice points in $\mathbb{R}^n$, and showed also, on every LCA group G, that every idempotent in $M(G)$ is concentrated on a compact subgroup of G. This reduced the problem to compact groups. I had some ideas on how to prove the conjecture when G is connected, in which case $\hat{G}$ has no elements of finite order, but before I could do any more, Paul Cohen proved the general case, in the same paper (Amer. J. Math. 82, 1960, 191-226) in which he made the first breakthrough on the so-called Littlewood problem.

To return for a moment to the functions φ that preserve $A(\mathbb{Z})$, they are exactly those whose graph is a member of the coset-ring of $\mathbb{Z} \times \mathbb{Z}$. This, too, has analogues with any LCA group in place of $\mathbb{T}$. For the gory details I refer to my book *Fourier Analysis on Groups*.

Cohen's proof was combinatorial and quite complicated. A much simpler one, using a weak-compactness argument, was later found by Ito and Amemiya (Bull. AMS 70, 1964, 774-776).

In Bull. AMS 69, 1963, 224-227 I studied idempotents in group algebras of (among other things) finite groups. Convolution of complex-valued functions is now defined by

$$(f * g)(x) = \sum_{y \in G} f(xy^{-1}) g(y).$$

For example, if G has order n and $f(x) = 1/n$ at all x in G, then $f*f = f$. Several interesting differences between abelian and nonabelian groups emerged. To mention just one, if G is abelian, of order n, then there are precisely 2^n idempotents in its group agebra, but on the nonabelian group of order 6 there are continuum many!

My last paper on this subject (Duke Math. J. 31, 1964, 585-602, joint with Hans Schneider) was purely algebraic, dealing with functions on groups with values in some ring.

Having mentioned the Littlewood problem, I should say something about it. Define

$$L_n = \inf \int_{-\pi}^{\pi} |e^{ik_1\theta} + \cdots + e^{ik_n\theta}| \frac{d\theta}{2\pi}$$

the infimum being taken over all n-tuples of distinct integers k_j. When the k_j form an arithmetic progression then the integral is $\sim (4/\pi^2) \log n$. (It is $< \sqrt{n}$ except when $n = 1$.) The question was whether

$$L_n > C \log n$$

for some universal $C > 0$.

This is a question about norms of certain idempotents in $M(\mathbb{T})$, because the Fourier coefficients of the measure

$$(e^{ik_1\theta} + \cdots + e^{ik_n\theta}) \frac{d\theta}{2\pi}$$

are 1 at $k_1, \cdots, k_n$ and are 0 elsewhere.

I suggested this problem to Paul while we were both in Rochester. At that time it was not even known that L_n is unbounded. Next fall he was at M.I.T., I was at Yale, and one evening he showed up, totally excited and bubbling over, and tried to explain to me, at twice his usual rapid-fire rate, that he had proved

$$L_n > (c \log n / \log \log n)^{1/8}.$$

I couldn't follow him at all, and finally told him: "Paul, go home, write it all down, and send it to me." Which he did.

Using Cohen's method, Davenport replaced 1/8 by 1/4. Later, Pichorides and Fournier (independently) obtained $L_n > (c \log n)^{1/2}$. The full conjecture was proved by Brent Smith (Annals of Math. 113, 1981, 613-618) by a simple but very ingenious argument that used nothing from the preceding papers. He obtained

$$L_n > \frac{1}{30} \log n.$$

His proof can be presented, in full detail, in one lecture. I have done it.

Stegeman (Math. Annalen 261, 1982, 51-54) refined that proof a bit, to

$$L_n > (4/\pi^3) \log n.$$

Whether arithmetic progressions give the minimum is not known.

CHAPTER 26

Riemann Sums

In this chapter, L^1 will refer to integration over the unit interval, and all functions that occur will be defined on the real line and will have period $1 : f(x) = f(x + 1)$ for all x.

Some time in 1962, during one of the Department's weekly post-colloquium parties, we sat around on the floor of Marvin Knopp's apartment in University Houses, drinking, when Anatole Beck, who was teaching Lebesgue integration, made the following

CONJECTURE. *The Riemann sums of f, namely, the averages*

$$(M_n f)(x) = \frac{1}{n} \sum_{k=1}^{n} f(x + \frac{k}{n})$$

converge to $\int_0^1 f(t)dt$ at almost every x.

I objected immediately and loudly that this couldn't possibly be true. We argued for a while and then made a *big* bet: $20, to be spent on a party by the winner. If I produced a counter-example within a year, I won. If not, I lost.

Next morning I remembered the most elementary theorem on dio-phantine approximation: to every irrational x correspond infinitely many rational numbers $r = p/q$ (p and q are integers) such that $|x - r| < q^{-2}$. Using this, it is easy to see that if $\frac{1}{2} < \alpha < 1$ and $f(x) = |x|^{-\alpha}$ on $[-\frac{1}{2}, \frac{1}{2}]$ then f is in L^1, but

$$\limsup_{n \to \infty}(M_n f)(x) = +\infty$$

at every irrational x.

So I had my counter-example. But Anatole insisted that he had only been talking about *bounded* functions. Since no one who had listened to us could or would remember exactly what was said, and since I wasn't quite sure myself, I accepted the challenge to find a bounded counter-example. Thinking about it off and on, it took me almost a year to produce one, but the effort was definitely worth while.

I knew the following theorem of Jessen (Annals of Math. 35, 1934, 248-251) which gives a positive result for certain subsequences:

If $\{n_i\}$ is an increasing sequence of positive integers in which each n_i is a divisor of n_{i+1} then, for every f in L^1,

$$\lim_{i \to \infty} (M_{n_i} f)(x) = \int_0^1 f(t)dt$$

at almost every x.

(When $n_i = a^i$ for some $a > 1$, this is a special case of Birkhoff's ergodic theorem. Jessen's theorem is the only gap theorem I know in which divisibility plays a role.) To win my bet I therefore had to avoid divisibility. Here is a simplified version of what I finally came up with, in Proc. AMS 15, 1964, 321-324.

THEOREM. *If $\{p_i\}$ is an increasing sequence of primes, and $\epsilon > 0$, then there is a measurable f such that $0 \le f \le 1$, $\int_0^1 f(t)dt < \epsilon$, but*

$$\limsup_{i \to \infty} (M_{p_i} f)(x) \ge \frac{1}{2}$$

at every x.

The proof actually produces such an f which is the characteristic function of an open set.

An interesting fact (a consequence of Dirichlet's theorem about primes in arithmetic progressions) is that there exist sequences $\{n_i\}$ which satisfy Jessen's hypothesis whereas the shifted sequences $\{1 + n_i\}$ consist entirely of primes. What matters here is thus not the rapidity with which a sequence $\{n_i\}$ tends to ∞, but rather its arithmetic structure. This unexpected delicate number-theoretic aspect of the behavior of $\{M_n f\}$ pleased me much more than just winning the bet.

Later, J. M. Marstrand (Proc. London Math. Soc. 21, 1970, 540-556) solved a similar problem (a harder one, in my opinion) by showing that there exist bounded measurable functions f for which the averages

$$\frac{1}{n} \sum_{k=1}^{n} f(kx)$$

do not converge to $\int_0^1 f(t)dt$. This disproved a 1923 conjecture made by Khinchine. Here, too, number theory played a role, as was the case in the only other papers on this subject that I have seen: one by M. Yu. Fominikh (Sov. Math. Izv. Vuz 29, #4, 1985, 81-93) and one by Révész and Rusza in Glasgow J. Math. 33, 1991, 129-134.

CHAPTER 27

Power Series with Gaps

Roughly speaking, these are power series of the form

$$(*) \qquad\qquad f(z) = \sum_{k=1}^{\infty} c_k z^{n_k}$$

where $\{n_k\}$ is a sequence of nonegative integers in which n_{k+1} is much larger than n_k. This topic has two aspects. First, given some information about $\{n_k\}$, what properties of f can be deduced from that? Secondly, gap series are very useful for constructing interesting (often pathological) functions.

The oldest example of the first kind is probably the theorem of Hadamard which says that if $n_{k+1}/n_k > \lambda$ for some $\lambda > 1$ and all k, then the circle of convergence of every series $(*)$ is also its natural boundary. For that reason, $\{n_k\}$ is called a *Hadamard set* if $n_{k+1}/n_k > \lambda > 1$ for all k. Series with such gaps have also been called *lacunary*.

The "high indices theorem" of Hardy and Littlewood (1926) states that if a lacunary series $(*)$ has $\lim f(r) = L$ as $r \nearrow 1$ then the series $\sum c_k$ converges and its sum is L. For this conclusion, no weaker gap condition will do: If

$$\liminf_{k \to \infty} n_{k+1}/n_k = 1$$

then there is a function of the form $(*)$ that is monotonic and bounded on the segment $[0,1)$ although $\sum c_k$ diverges (Proc. AMS 17, 1966, 434-435). In fact, the c_k's can be unbounded. This is probably the easiest theorem I ever proved. I did it while proctoring an hour exam.

Next, let us call a set E a *Paley set* if E is the union of finitely many Hadamard sets; equivalently, if the number of terms of E between x and $2x$ stays bounded as $x \to \infty$. Paley proved in 1933 that if $f(z) = \sum a_n z^n$

lies in the Hardy space H^1 and E is a Paley set, then

$$\sum_{n \in E} |a_n|^2 < \infty.$$

In J. London Math. Soc. 33, 1957, 307-311, I showed that this conclusion holds *only* for Paley sets. We thus have an equivalence between an analytic property of a set E (f in H^1 implies the convergence of the above series) and a structural one (a bound on the number of terms between x and $2x$).

This result extends to discrete ordered abelian groups in place of the integers.

Paley sets also play an interesting role in the context of H^p-spaces in the unit ball of $\mathbb{C}^n$. A number of such theorems are in Indiana Univ. Math. J. 37, 1988, 255-275, a joint paper with Pat Ahern.

The construction of gap series with desired properties often proceeds by induction: having $n_1, \cdots n_p$ and $c_1, \cdots c_p$, choose n_{p+1} so large that something happens that you want to happen, then choose c_{p+1} and continue.

In this way Lohwater, Piranian, and I (in Math. Scand. 3, 1955, 103-106) showed that for a suitable sequence $\{n_k\}$ the function

$$f(z) = \int_0^z \exp\{\frac{1}{2} \sum_{k=1}^{\infty} w^{n_k}\} dw$$

is one-to-one on the closed unit disc $\overline{U}$, its Taylor series converges absolutely (hence uniformly) on $\overline{U}$, but its derivative oscillates so violently near the boundary of U that

$$\limsup |f'(re^{i\theta})| + \infty, \quad \liminf |f'(re^{i\theta})| = 0$$

$$\limsup \arg f'(re^{i\theta}) = +\infty, \quad \liminf \arg f'(re^{i\theta}) = -\infty$$

for almost every θ as $r \nearrow 1$.

Gap series also play a role in my proof that different H^p-spaces in the unit ball B of $\mathbb{C}^n (n > 1)$ have different zero-sets (Indag. Math. 38, 1976, 57-65). In fact, for every $p(0 < p < \infty)$ there is an f in $H^p(B)$, $f \not\equiv 0$, whose zero-set $Z(f)$ has the following property: If $q > p$, h is in $H^q(B)$, and $Z(h) \supset Z(f)$, then $h \equiv 0$.

For the next example, call a continuous curve $\gamma : [0,1) \to U$ a *boundary path* if $|\gamma(t)| \to 1$ as $t \nearrow 1$.

If $n_k = (k!)^2$ and $g(z) = \sum_{k=1}^{\infty} k^{-1} z^{n_k}$ then g maps every boundary path onto a curve of infinite length.

The reason is that $(k!)^2$ increases so rapidly that there are disjoint annuli
$$A_k = \{z : 1 - \frac{2}{n_k} < |z| < 1 - \frac{1}{n_k}\}$$
on which the k-th term of the Taylor series of $g'(z)$ dominates the sum of the others: there is a constant $c > 0$ such that $|g'(z)| > ck^{-1}n_k$ on A_k. The total variation of g on any curve that crosses A_k is therefore larger than c/k, and $\sum_k c/k = \infty$.

(For an update on these matters, see Pommerenke, Math. Z. 187, 1984, 165-170, and the references cited there.)

This g maps U onto a Riemann surface S. Since g is in H^2 it has finite radial limits at almost every boundary point. The images of these radii are thus nonrectifiable curves that end at some "boundary point" of S. But if you start at some point of S and follow a straight-line path you hit no boundary point, you stay on S all the way to ∞, otherwise the inverse image of some *bounded* interval would be a boundary path in U, a contradiction. I have tried to visualize what S looks like but have not come up with a clear picture.

In Duke Math. J. 22, 1955, 235-242 I used a similar g to prove:

THEOREM. *There is a bounded holomorphic f in U for which the set*
$$Q_f = \{\theta : \int_0^1 |f'(re^{i\theta})|dr < \infty\}$$
has measure 0 and is of the first Baire category.

The proof used the fact that $g = g_1/g_2$, a quotient of two H^∞-functions, and that for all but countably many constants α the function $f = g_1 + \alpha g_2$ has Q_f of measure 0. "First category" then comes for free, because the integral is a lower semicontinuous function of θ. One can even get inner functions and functions in the disc algebra for which Q_f is equally small.

Geometrically, Q_f is the set of all θ such that f maps the radius ending at $e^{i\theta}$ onto a curve of finite length.

For over 36 years it remained a nagging open problem to decide whether Q_f could be empty for some f in H^∞. I couldn't even conjecture which way it might go. I know that quite a few people worked on it. At my retirement conference, in 1991, I offered a prize for this problem. It was solved by Jean Bourgain (Duke Math. J. 69, 1993, 671-682) in an astonishing way. He proved not only that Q_f cannot be empty if f is in H^∞, but that Q_f must be large in the sense that its Hausdorff dimension is 1. And, unlike everybody else who had attacked this, he used no ideas coming from geometric function theory but worked directly with the Taylor series of f.

CHAPTER 28

Trigonometric Series with Gaps

This is the title of one of my favorite papers (J. Math. Mech. 9, 1960, 203-228). Usually, as soon as I prove a theorem I write it up, send it off, and start thinking about something else. But this paper I let ripen and grow for at least two years. Its background consists of two classical theorems about trigonometric series of the form

$$(*) \qquad \sum_{k=1}^{\infty} (a_k \cos n_k \theta + b_k \sin n_k \theta)$$

in which $n_{k+1}/n_k > \lambda$ for some $\lambda > 1$ and all k. (So $\{n_k\}$ is a Hadamard set, as defined in the preceding chapter.)

(1) If $(*)$ is the Fourier series of a bounded function then

$$\sum_{1}^{\infty} (|a_k| + |b_k|) < \infty.$$

(Sidon, Math. Annalen 97, 1927, 675-676.)

(2) If $(*)$ is the Fourier series of some f in L^1 then f is in L^p for all $p < \infty$. (Banach, Studia Math. 2, 1930, 207-220.)

The closed graph theorem shows that the conclusions of (1) and (2) are equivalent, respectively, to the existence of constants B and A_p such that

$$\sum (|a_k| + |b_k|) \le B\|f\|_\infty \quad \text{and} \quad \|f\|_p \le A_p \|f\|_1$$

for all f whose Fourier coefficients are 0 off the given set $\{n_k\}$.

Here, as usual, $\|f\|_p = \{\int_{-\pi}^{\pi} |f(e^{i\theta})|^p d\theta/2\pi\}^{1/p}$ if $0 < p < \infty$, and $\|f\|_\infty$ is the (essential) supremum of $|f|$ on the unit circle.

If E is a set of integers, not necessarily positive, an f in L^1 will be called an E-function if its Fourier coefficients

$$\hat{f}(n) = \frac{1}{2\pi} \int_{-\pi}^{\pi} f(e^{i\theta}) e^{-in\theta} d\theta$$

175

are 0 at every integer n outside E. A trignometric polynomial that is an E-function will be called an E-polynomial. (1) and (2) lead to two definitions:

(i) Motivated by (1), E is called a *Sidon set* if there is a constant $B < \infty$ such that

$$\sum_{-\infty}^{\infty} |\hat{f}(n)| \le B\|f\|_\infty$$

for every E-polynomial f.

(ii) I defined E to be a $\Lambda(p)$-*set* $(0 < p < \infty)$ if to every positive $r < p$ corresponds a constant $A_{r,p} < \infty$ such that

$$\|f\|_p \le A_{r,p}\|f\|_r$$

for every E-polynomial f. (It is an easy consequence of Hölder's inequality that if this holds for just one $r < p$ then it holds for every $r < p$.)

In this terminology, the above-mentioned classical theorems say that Hadamard sets are Sidon, as well as $\Lambda(p)$ for all $p < \infty$. Definitions (i) and (ii) describe analytic properties of E. The problem was to correlate them with structural properties.

Before turning to these it should be mentioned that the analytic properties can easily be restated in several ways, using some basic functional analysis. For instance, E is Sidon if and only if every bounded function on E is the restriction to E of the Fourier transform of some μ in $M(\mathbb{T})$.

Now let $n_1, n_2, n_3, \ldots$ be an enumeration of the terms of E (which, I repeat, may contain both positive and negative integers) and let $R_s(E, n)$ be the number of ways of representing n in the form

$$n = \pm n_{k_1} \pm n_{k_2} \pm \cdots \pm n_{k_s} \quad (k_1 < k_2 < \cdots < k_s).$$

For instance, if $n_k = 3^k$ then $R_s(E, n) \le 1$ for all n and all $s \ge 1$.

Using this notion, I obtained a sufficient condition for Sidonicity which was weaker than similar ones due to Stečkin and Hewitt. My student Dan Rider went much further (Can. J. Math. 18, 1966, 389-398). He removed more than half of my hypotheses and reached a stronger conclusion:

THEOREM (Rider). *If* $E = E_1 \cup E_2 \cup \cdots \cup E_m$ *and if there is a constant* $B < \infty$ *such that*

$$R_s(E_i, 0) \le B^s$$

for $i = 1, 2, \cdots m$ and $s = 1, 2, 3, \cdots$, then $E \cup (-E)$ is a Sidon set.

Consequently, finite unions of Hadamard sets are Sidon. But not all Sidon sets are such unions.

In the opposite direction I proved:

THEOREM. *If E is a Sidon set then there is a $C < \infty$ such that no arithmetic progression of N terms contains more than $C \log N$ terms of E.*

A similar result, also involving arithmetic progressions, holds for $\Lambda(p)$:

THEOREM. *If $p > 2$ and E is a $\Lambda(p)$-set then there is a $C < \infty$ such that no arithmetic progression of N terms contains more than $CN^{2/p}$ terms of E.*

If E is a $\Lambda(1)$-set then there is a $C < \infty$ such that E contains no arithmetic progression of more than C terms.

There is an interesting relation between Sidon and $\Lambda(p)$:

THEOREM. (a) *Every Sidon set is $\Lambda(p)$ for all $p < \infty$.*

(b) *More precisely, if $\sum |\hat{f}(n)| \le B\|f\|_\infty$ for every E-polynomial f, then*

$$\|g\|_p \le B\sqrt{p}\|g\|_2$$

for all E-polynomials g and all $p > 2$.

I showed also that the converse of (a) is false: Some sets are $\Lambda(p)$ for all $p < \infty$ without being Sidon. As regards (b), I showed that $\sqrt{p}$ could not be replaced by any function of p that grows more slowly, as $p \to \infty$, but I did not prove or disprove the converse of (b). That was done by Gilles Pisier (C. R. Acad. Sci. Paris A 286, 1978, 671-674):

THEOREM (Pisier). *If there is a $B < \infty$ such that*

$$\|g\|_p \le B\sqrt{p}\|g\|_2$$

for all $p > 2$ and all E-polynomials g, then E is a Sidon set.

His proof used techniques that were definitely not in my repertoire.

It is an immediate consequence of the definition of $\Lambda(p)$ that every $\Lambda(q)$-set is also $\Lambda(p)$ when $p < q$. The conjecture arose, naturally, that this inclusion is always proper. To make this more precise, let us look at two properties which a positive number p may or may not have.

$X(p)$: There is a $\Lambda(p)$-set which is $\Lambda(q)$ for no $q > p$.
$Y(p)$: Given $q > p$ there is a $\Lambda(p)$-set which is not $\Lambda(q)$.

Of course, $X(p)$ implies $Y(p)$. Here is what is known about them:

THEOREM. (a) $X(p)$ *is true if* $p > 2$.
(b) $X(p)$ *fails if* $0 < p < 2$.

The status of $X(2)$ and of $Y(p)$ for $p < 2$ is still unknown.

I proved only a very special case of (a), namely the case of even integers $p \geq 4$. My proof used combinatorics which, I believe, I learned from Salem's M.I.T. lectures.

Part (b) was first proved by Bachelis and Ebenstein (Pac. J. Math. 54, 1974, 35-58) for $1 \leq p < 2$. Katherine Hare (Proc. AMS 104, 1988, 829-834) extended it to $0 < p < 2$, with a more elementary proof.

Almost 30 years after my paper was written, Bourgain (Acta Math. 162, 1989, 227-245) proved all of (a), as a consequence of a theorem about uniformly bounded sets of orthogonal functions. He has told me that he regards this as the most difficult problem he has ever solved, and he was quite disappointed that $\Lambda(p)$-sets were not mentioned in the lecture (given by Caffarelli) that described the work for which he won his Fields medal, at the Zürich Congress in 1994.

Most of the results described here have been extended from the integers to arbitrary discrete abelian groups, and beyond. The book "Sidon Sets" by Lopez and Ross (1975) has lots of further information, not only about Sidon sets, but also about $\Lambda(p)$.

CHAPTER 29

Function Theory in Polydiscs

I am often asked why I left harmonic analysis and switched to several complex variables. One answer is that I had written my 1962 book *Fourier Series on Groups* which pretty much wrapped up what was known at the time about analysis on locally compact abelian groups. My timing was fortunate – I could include Malliavin's negative solution of the spectral synthesis problem. Of the open questions that were still around, some seemed too hard and the others didn't attract me much.

A second answer is that I didn't really leave, because when studying holomorphic functions in the polydisc $U^n = U \times \cdots \times U$ much of the action takes place on its distinguished boundary, the torus $\mathbb{T}^n = \mathbb{T} \times \cdots \times \mathbb{T}$, where one runs into multiple Fourier series.

But the right answer is the third. Some time, probably in the fall of 1963, I noticed two papers, back to back in the February 1962 issue of Proc. AMS, the first by Bojanic and Stoll, the second by Bochner. The first proved that if $f : \mathbb{C}^n \to \mathbb{C}$ is holomorphic, and $|f(z)| = 1$ at every z on $\mathbb{T}^n$, then f is a monomial. Reading between the lines of the second it seemed to me that Bochner might have been the referee of the first; he gave a better proof, one that also worked for other circular sets in place of $\mathbb{T}^n$ (with an appropriately different conclusion). The fact that three mathematicians, one of them Bochner, published such a theorem in AD 1962 made me think that there must be a lot of easy theorems in that area that had not been proved, simply because no one had asked the right questions.

Lee Stout had finished his dissertation but was going to stay in Madison over the spring semester, and I suggested to him that we try to find out what the analogues of finite Blaschke products were in U^n. Calling a holomorphic function $f : U^n \to U$ *inner* if the radial limits of $|f|$ are 1 at almost every point of $\mathbb{T}^n$, another way of stating the problem was: Find all inner function in U^n that belong to the *polydisc algebra* $A(U^n)$, the set of all f in $C(\overline{U}^n)$ that are holomorphic in U^n.

We found a complete answer (J. Math. Mech. 14, 1965, 991-1006): Let $Q(z) = Q(z_1, \cdots, z_n)$ be a polynomial with no zeros on $\overline{U}^n$ and let $M(z) = z_1^{\alpha_1} \cdots z_n^{\alpha_n}$ be a monomial, so chosen that

$$P(z) = M(z)\tilde{Q}(1/z_1, \cdots, 1/z_n)$$

is a polynomial. ($\tilde{Q}$ is obtained from Q by replacing each coefficient by its complex conjugate.) Since $1/z_j = \bar{z}_j$ on $\mathbb{T}^n$, P/Q is inner, and it is obviously in $A(U^n)$. The nonobvious converse is that *every inner function in $A(U^n)$ is obtained this way.*

If one merely requires Q to have no zeros in U^n (rather than on $\overline{U}^n$) this recipe produces every *rational* inner function in U^n.

Beyond the rational ones there is a vast and uncharted jungle of inner functions in U^n. Some of these were discussed later, in Duke Math. J. 39, 1972, 767-777, my first joint paper with Pat Ahern.

During the next few years my aim was to see how much of our extremely detailed knowledge about holomorphic functions in U (such as boundary values, distribution of zeros as related to growth restrictions, factorization theorems, invariant subspaces, interpolation theorems) can be carried over to U^n. As was to be expected, I found some analogues, some counter examples, and some genuinely new theorems whose one-variable versions either make no sense or reduce to trivialities. Much of this work was done in 1966-67, on leave in La Jolla.

My 1969 book *Function Theory in Polydiscs* contains the results of that research. Since I had all the material at my finger tips this book was very easy to write. It only took me about two months. Here are some samples from it.

(1) *If f is holomorphic in U^n and no point of $\mathbb{T}^n$ is a limit point of zeros of f in U^n, then f has the same zeros as some bounded holomorphic function, i.e., there is a zero-free g, holomorphic in U^n, such that fg is in $H^\infty(U^n)$.*

One remarkable feature of this is that $H^\infty(U^n)$ cannot be replaced by $A(U^n)$ in the conclusion.

I don't remember what made me think of such a theorem. I do remember that I first had a proof that worked only for $n = 2$, and that I tried to convince myself that it was false for $n \geq 3$. But after a while I found a proof of the general case, and have no idea what my first one could have been.

Wondering what would happen to this if U^n were enlarged until it was all of $\mathbb{C}^n$ led me to a geometric characterization of algebraic varieties (J. Math. Mech. 17, 1968, 671-684).

(2) Let D be the *diagonal* of U^n, the set of all $z = (z_1, \cdots z_n)$ in U^n for which $z_1 = z_2 = \cdots = z_n$. Thus D is a copy of U, embedded in U^n, whose boundary lies in $\mathbb{T}^n$.

If f is in $A(U^n)$ and f has no zero on $\mathbb{T}^n \cup D$, then f has no zero at any point of $\overline{U}^n$.

The point is that $\mathbb{T}^n \cup D$ is a very small set, compared to U^n, especially when n is large. The theorem is also true if D is replaced by certain other embeddings of U.

This turned out to be my contribution to applied mathematics. In a 1979 report issued by Philips Research Labs in Brussels, Belgium, the theorem is called a "cornerstone" in multivariable stability theory.

Don't ask me why.

(3) The most difficult theorem in this book is due to Frank Forelli (J. Math. Mech. 17, 1968, 1073-1086). It concerns a property (which he called "S-width zero") of compact subsets of $\mathbb{T}^n$ which implies that they are interpolation sets for $A(U^n)$.

(4) In one variable, every f in $H^1(U)$ is a product of two functions in $H^2(U)$ – a very useful factorization theorem, especially since the factors in $f = gh$ can be so chosen that their norms satisfy $\|g\|_2^2 = \|h\|_2^2 = \|f\|_1$. The following terminology will make it easy to describe how the corresponding n-variable problem was solved.

For Banach spaces X, Y, Z, call a map $\varphi : X \times Y \to Z$ *open at the origin* if the image of every neighborhood of $(0,0)$ in $X \times Y$ contains a neighborhood of 0 in Z.

Let $\mu_n : H^2(U^n) \times H^2(U^n) \to H^1(U^n)$ be the multiplication map that sends each pair (g, h) to its product gh.

Thus μ_1 is surjective and open at the origin. I could prove that μ_n is not open at the origin if $n \geq 3$ and deduced from this that μ_n is not surjective if $n \geq 4$. Joe Miles (Proc. AMS 52, 1975, 319-322) lowered these dimensions by 1, and Jean-Pierre Rosay (Ill. J. Math. 19, 1975, 479-482) finished it up (using Miles' result) by showing that μ_2 is not surjective. This factorization theorem is thus true only when $n = 1$.

It occurred to me to ask, for general Banach spaces, whether every continuous surjective bilinear $\varphi : X \times Y \to Z$ must be open at the origin (as it is for linear maps). I thought that this might be familiar to experts in certain areas of functional analysis, such as tensor products, but nobody seemed to know anything about it until Paul Cohen produced an intricate counter example, with $X = Y = Z = \ell^1$ (J. Functional Anal. 16, 1974, 235-240). When I mentioned this in class one day, a student asked: "What about the finite-dimensional case?" I must have answered something like "I suppose it is true but I have no proof". A couple of days later, Charles Horowitz, a new instructor, came in with a bilinear map from $\mathbb{C}^3 \times \mathbb{C}^3$ *onto* $\mathbb{C}^4$ which was not open at the origin. His proof, in Proc. AMS 53, 1975, 293-294, takes about half a page!

(5) The automorphisms of U^n are described explicitly, and the proper holomorphic maps from U^k to U^n are discussed in some detail.

CHAPTER 30

Function Theory in Balls

The polydiscs U^n are one natural generalization of the unit disc in $\mathbb{C}$. Another, just as natural, are the unit balls B in $\mathbb{C}^n$, for $n \geq 2$, where

$$B = \{z = (z_1, \cdots, z_n) : |z_1|^2 + \cdots + |z_n|^2 < 1\}.$$

(I write B, not B^n, since B^n looks like the product of n copies of B. When it is desirable to be explicit about the dimension, I prefer B_n.) But whereas it was very easy to get started in U^n, B was quite resistant. Sometime in the early seventies I was invited to give 3 or 4 lectures at McGill University in Montreal. When I arrived, Drury (best known, at least to me, for having proved that the union of any two Sidon sets is Sidon) asked me what I was going to talk about. When I said about the ball in $\mathbb{C}^n$, his reply was: "But nothing is known about the ball!" He was almost right.

I don't know just what broke the ice. It may have been Korányi's theorem in Trans. AMS 135, 1969, 507-516 which, quite unexpectedly, showed not only that the analogue of Fatou's theorem is true in B (which is obvious for radial limits), but whereas in U the admissible approach regions are angular, in B they are larger, they have second-order contact with the boundary of B in the complex-tangential directions. I remember Zygmund shaking his head over this, wondering how it was possible to get a better theorem in several variables than is true in one.

The following may give a hint of what goes on here.

Take $n = 2$, let $f : B \to U$ be holomorphic, and look at the partial derivatives of f at a point $p = (r, 0), 0 < r < 1$. Put $\delta = 1 - r^2$. Then $|(\partial f/\partial z_1)(p)|$ can be as large as $1/\delta$. Since (r, λ) lies in B when $|\lambda| < \sqrt{\delta}$, the one-variable Schwarz lemma shows that $|(\partial f/\partial z_2)(p)| \leq 1/\sqrt{\delta}$, which is much smaller than $1/\delta$ when r is close to 1. So, roughly speaking, f varies more slowly near the boundary point $(1, 0)$ in the z_2-direction than it can vary in the z_1-direction. This does not prove

Korànyi's theorem, but it shows that not all directions are equal, that there are "nonisotropic" phenomena.

These were also shown to exist at the boundaries of strictly pseudoconvex regions, whose study took off as soon as the Henkin-Ramirez integral formulas became known.

In a paper on "Spaces of Type $H^\infty + C$" (Ann. Inst. Fourier 25, 1975, 99-125) which deals with some harmonic analysis topics and also with U^n and B, I learned to integrate over spheres. During the next few years I solved several problems in B, learned what others were doing there, and wrote *Function Theory in the Unit Ball of* $\mathbb{C}^n$, published in 1980.

The most difficult chapter in that book is devoted to the Henkin-Skoda theorem which characterizes the zero-sets of functions belonging to the Nevanlinna class in B, by an analogue of the Blaschke condition (which does it when $n = 1$). Henkin and Skoda had worked independently, in Russia and France, respectively, but their proofs are remarkably similar. They worked in strictly pseudoconvex regions, using methods and techniques that were quite unfamiliar to me. I tried to decipher these papers step by step, to see how things would simplify in the ball, kept telling myself "if this means anything it must mean such and such" and, having proved many "such and suches" finally managed to put the pieces together in a way that I could understand.

I won't describe the contents of this book any further – it covers a lot of territory – expect for the last chapter, most of which is devoted to my conjecture that there exists no nonconstant inner function in B when $n \geq 2$, and to several closely related conjectures.

As in U or U^n, a holomorphic $f : B \to U$ is defined to be inner if

$$\lim_{r \nearrow 1} |f(r\zeta)| = 1$$

at almost every ζ on the sphere S that bounds B. Here "almost every" refers to the positive rotation-invariant measure σ on S, normalized so that $\sigma(S) = 1$.

I made this conjecture because I could prove, on the one hand, that *every* such f is extremely oscillatory near *every* point of S, but, on the other hand, that the boundary values of f are so well-behaved that they induce a measure-preserving map from S to $\mathbb{T}$, if $f(0) = 0$.

This conjecture became well known, and most of those who thought about it seemed to believe it. I think that Frank Forelli was the only one who made any progress toward proving it. Call a measure on S an RP-measure if its Poisson integral is the real part of a holomorphic function. We noticed that the inner function conjecture would follow if one could show that no RP-measure is singular with respect to σ. For certain classes of RP-measures Frank actually proved more: they were absolutely continuous with respect to σ.

In the summer of 1981 A. B. Aleksandrov (a young member of the highly productive group of Leningrad analysts which is now dispersed in several countries) sent me a letter with a theorem similar to the one stated below (the positivity of μ was missing) which came close to producing inner functions in B. Frank and I joked that we had better hurry up and prove the conjecture before Aleksandrov could prove the opposite.

In November came the the the real surprise:

THEOREM (Aleksandrov). *If φ is a positive lower semicontinuous function on S, and φ is in $L^1(\sigma)$, then there is a positive measure μ on S, singular with respect to σ, such that $\varphi d\sigma - d\mu$ is an RP-measure.*

What does this have to do with inner functions? Well, take some g in $C(\overline{B})$, holomorphic in B, $|g| < 1$, and apply the theorem to $\varphi = -\log|g|$. This gives a holomorphic h in B whose real part is the Poisson integral of $\varphi d\sigma - d\mu$. Put

$$f = ge^h.$$

Since $\mu \geq 0$, f is bounded in B. Since μ is singular,

$$|f| = |g|e^{\mathrm{Re}h} = |g|e^{\varphi} = 1 \quad \text{a.e. on} \quad S.$$

So f is inner. As an added bonus, f has the same zeros as the given function g.

Aleksandrov sent me several more letters, with further developments. I found this quite remarkable, because sending scientific information out of the Soviet Union could be a risky business in the years before Gorbachev. When my book was translated into Russian he rewrote the last chapter.

Returning to Aleksandrov's "modification theorem" (so called because μ "modifies" φ), I had proved a theorem just like it (in Bull. AMS 73, 1967, 369-371) with $\mathbb{T}^n$ and U^n in place of S and B, basically by pushing Fourier coefficients around. It had never occurred to me to try this on S. Even if it had, I might not have succeeded, it was much harder on S than on $\mathbb{T}^n$. (I published two more papers on such modifications, in the context of harmonic analysis, in Proc. AMS 19, 1968, 1069-1074, and in Bull. AMS 74, 1968, 526-528.)

The existence of inner functions was also proved by Erik Löw in Norway, independently, a few weeks after Aleksandrov did it, by pushing an earlier construction of Hakim and Sibony a bit further than they had done.

It soon became clear that inner functions could not be as useful in B as they are in U, but the techniques that were developed to prove their existence could be used successfully to prove a variety of existence theorems for holomorphic functions f with the boundary values of $|f|$ or of $\mathrm{Re}\, f$ prescribed on S (almost everywhere or in some other approximate sense) and which can also be made to satisfy various additional interpolation data and growth restrictions in B. These developments formed the content of a CBMS Conference in 1985 in which I was the principal lecturer. The resulting publication is No. 63 in the *Regional Conference Series in Mathematics*, published by AMS.

Among my later work on B there is one paper that I feel I must mention. It involves the automorphisms of B and the so-called invariant Laplacian $\tilde{\Delta}$.

The automorphisms of B are, naturally, the one-to-one holomorphic maps from B onto B. They form a group, $\mathrm{Aut}(B)$. Every ψ in $\mathrm{Aut}(B)$ is a composition of a unitary operator on $\mathbb{C}^n$ and an involution φ_a of the form

$$\varphi_a(z) = \frac{a - Pz - (1 - \langle a, a\rangle)^{1/2} Qz}{1 - \langle z, a\rangle}$$

where a is in B, P is the orthogonal projection of $\mathbb{C}^n$ onto the subspace spanned by a, $Qz = z - Pz$, and $\langle z, a\rangle = \sum_1^n z_j \bar{a}_j$.

$\tilde{\Delta}$ is the differential operator which coincides with the ordinary Laplacian at the origin, and commutes with the action of $\mathrm{Aut}(B)$: for every f in $C^2(B)$ and every ψ in $\mathrm{Aut}(B)$,

$$(\tilde{\Delta}f) \circ \psi = \tilde{\Delta}(f \circ \psi).$$

The φ_a's remind one of the Moebius transformations of U (when $n = 1, Pz = z, Q = 0$). The functions that satisfy

$$\tilde{\Delta}f = 0$$

are therefore call $\mathcal{M}$-harmonic. If f is $\mathcal{M}$-harmonic, so is $f \circ \psi$, for every ψ in $\mathrm{Aut}(B)$.

Let ν be Lebesgue measure on $\mathbb{C}^n$, so normalized that $\nu(B) = 1$. If f is $\mathcal{M}$-harmonic and is in $L^1(\nu)$ then f has the mean-value property

$$(*) \qquad \int_B (f \circ \psi)\, d\nu = f(\psi(0))$$

for every ψ in Aut(B).

As regards a possible converse, Pat Ahern and I asked the following

QUESTION. If f is in $L^1(\nu)$ and $(*)$ holds for every ψ in Aut(B), must f then be $\mathcal{M}$-harmonic?

This was unknown even for $n = 1$. Together with Manuel Flores, a student, we found the following unexpected answer (J. Funct. Anal. 111, 1993, 380–397):

Yes if $n \leq 11$, no if $n \geq 12$.

(However, if L^1 is replaced by L^∞, the answer is yes for all n.)

How can one arrive at such an answer? We began of course by trying to prove "yes" for all n. We introduced a family of linear operators which led to very explicit entire functions Φ_n of one variable, one for each n, and reduced the problem to showing that Φ_n has no zero in the strip $-1 < \operatorname{Re}\lambda < 0$. The argument principle showed then that this was true for all n below some threshold and false above it. To find where the change took place we did some computations on a hand-held calculator (its arctan button was very useful). Fortunately, the change occurred at a place that was within our reach. If it had happened between 357 and 358 we would have needed help from someone with a real computer.

Since $\tilde{\Delta}$ is the Laplace-Beltrami operator related to the Bergman metric on B, there ought to be something visible in the geometry of B_n that changes with n and that could explain our strange result. We have not found such an explanation.

CHAPTER 31

Holomorphic Maps from $\mathbb{C}^n$ to $\mathbb{C}^n$

Throughout this chapter, $n > 1$. To describe the first problems that Rosay and I began to work on when he arrived in Madison, call a discrete subset D of $\mathbb{C}^n$ *tame in* $\mathbb{C}^n$ if D can be "straightened" by an automorphism Φ of $\mathbb{C}^n$. More precisely, there should be a Φ in $\mathrm{Aut}(\mathbb{C}^n)$ that carries D onto an arithmetic progression. ($\mathrm{Aut}(\mathbb{C}^n)$ is of course the group of all one-to-one holomorphic maps from $\mathbb{C}^n$ onto $\mathbb{C}^n$. "Discrete" means, in this context, that no point of $\mathbb{C}^n$ is a limit point of D.)

I had earlier proved the following:

If $1 \le k < n$, π is a linear projection of $\mathbb{C}^n$ onto $\mathbb{C}^k$, and $\pi(D)$ is discrete in $\mathbb{C}^k$, then D is tame in $\mathbb{C}^n$. Moreover, if $\pi^{-1}(w) \cap D$ is a finite set for every w in $\mathbb{C}^k$, then D can be straightened by a volume-preserving Φ in $\mathrm{Aut}(\mathbb{C}^n)$.

(When the latter can be done, we call D *very tame in* $\mathbb{C}^n$.)

It follows that every discrete D in $\mathbb{C}^k$ is very tame in $\mathbb{C}^n$ if $k < n$. Also, every discrete D in $\mathbb{C}^n$ is a union of two that are very tame in $\mathbb{C}^n$.

It came therefore as a surprise when we proved (in Trans. AMS 310, 1988, 47-86, another favorite paper) that non-tame discrete sets exist in $\mathbb{C}^n$, and that not all tame sets are very tame. The main step in the proof showed that some such D's are "unavoidable" by nondegenerate holomorphic maps. This means that if $F : \mathbb{C}^n \to \mathbb{C}^n$ is holomorphic and its Jacobian is not identically 0, then $F(\mathbb{C}^n)$ must intersect D.

Similar techniques proved that some D's are "rigid", meaning that the identity map is the only automorphism of $\mathbb{C}^n$ that carries D onto D. As a corollary of the proof of this one can see that there are continuum many equivalence classes of discrete sets in $\mathbb{C}^n$, if we call two sets equivalent provided some Φ in $\mathrm{Aut}(\mathbb{C}^n)$ carries one onto the other.

On the other hand, all countable dense subsets of $\mathbb{C}^n$ are equivalent in this sense:

If X and Y are countable dense subsets of $\mathbb{C}^n$ then there is a volume-preserving Φ in $\mathrm{Aut}(\mathbb{C}^n)$ such that $\Phi(X) = Y$.

When I mention this in a lecture it often causes disbelief.

The same paper contains several new examples of Fatou-Bieberbach domains (these are open sets Ω in $\mathbb{C}^n$, $\Omega \neq \mathbb{C}^n$, which can be mapped onto $\mathbb{C}^n$ by a one-to-one holomorphic map), and it contains an example of a *locally* volume-preserving holomorphic $F : \mathbb{C}^n \to \mathbb{C}^n$ whose range $F(\mathbb{C}^n)$ has finite volume.

We used the ideas of this last example to show (in RIMS Kyoto Univ. 19, 1993, 161-166) that there are Fatou Bieberbach domains Ω (of necessarily infinite volume) such that the volume of $\Omega \cap rB$ grows arbitrarily slowly as $r \nearrow \infty$. Here rB is the ball of radius r, center 0.

The above-mentioned facts about discrete and countable dense sets show that $\mathrm{Aut}(\mathbb{C}^n)$ is a very complicated group for all $n \geq 2$. One way to get some insight into its structure would be to find out all about its finite subgroups, or, more modestly, about the finite cyclic ones, i.e., about the *periodic* automorphisms of $\mathbb{C}^n$.

It is easy to find the periodic *linear* ones, say of period m. After choosing an appropriate basis for $\mathbb{C}^n$, their matrix representations are diagonal, with m-th roots of unity as eigenvalues. If L is such a periodic linear map, and Φ is in $\mathrm{Aut}(\mathbb{C}^n)$, then $\Phi^{-1}L\Phi$ is also periodic. Pat Ahern and I tried to determine whether every periodic F in $\mathrm{Aut}(\mathbb{C}^n)$ is obtained in this way, i.e., whether every such F is conjugate, within $\mathrm{Aut}(\mathbb{C}^n)$, to a linear map.

In Indiana J. Math. 44, 1995, 287-300, we found a positive answer, but *only* when $n = 2$, and *only* when F is in the so-called *overshear subgroup* of $\mathrm{Aut}(\mathbb{C}^2)$.

On $\mathbb{C}^2$, an overshear is a map F of the form

$$F(z, w) = (z, we^{h(z)} + g(z)) \quad \text{or} \quad F(z, w) = (ze^{h(w)} + g(w), w)$$

where g and h are arbitrary entire functions of one variable. (This name was apparently coined by Lászlo Lempert.) When $h = 0$, these maps are called shears.

On $\mathbb{C}^n$, $n \geq 2$, let $z' = (z_1, \cdots z_{n-1})$, $z = (z', z_n)$. An overshear is then an F of the form

$$F(z) = F(z', z_n) = (z', z_n e^{h(z')} + g(z'))$$

where $g, h : \mathbb{C}^{n-1} \to \mathbb{C}$ are entire functions, followed (or preceded) by a permutation of the coordinates. Again, when $h \equiv 0$, F is a shear. Note that shears preserve volume.

In April 1988 I gave a lecture in Lund about these topics. At the end I mentioned a conjecture that Rosay and I had made: The volume-preserving automorphism F_0 of $\mathbb{C}^2$ given by

$$F_0(z, w) = (ze^{zw}, we^{-zw})$$

cannot be approximated, uniformly on compact subsets of $\mathbb{C}^2$, by finite compositions of shears. One reason for this was that F_0 preserves sets of the form $zw = \text{const.}$, which looked quite different from what shears can do, another was that the Taylor series of the components of F_0 did not seem to lend themselves to that kind of approximation.

A few weeks later I received a letter from Erik Andersén, a student who had been in the audience. He had misunderstood the conjecture and sent me a proof that F_0 was not a finite composition of shears. This did not surprise me, even though the proof was by no means trivial, but when I told him what our conjecture really was, he answered very quickly: "But that approximation I can do!" I had some questions about this, and after we had exchanged several letters, he had progressed from the special case of F_0 to the following splendid

THEOREM (ANDERSÉN). *Every volume-preserving automorphism of $\mathbb{C}^n$ is a limit, uniformly on compact subsets of $\mathbb{C}^n$, of a sequence of finite compositions of shears.*

This appeared in Complex Variables 14, 1990, 223-235. In a joint paper with Lempert (Invent. Math. 110, 1992, 371-388) they removed "volume-preserving" from the hypothesis and replaced "shears" by "over-shears" in the conclusion.

It's not often that a lecture leads to such beautiful results!

There are many open problems in this area. One of the most famous is the "Jacobian Conjecture" which says: If $F : \mathbb{C}^n \to \mathbb{C}^n$ is a *polynomial map* whose Jacobian is nowhere 0 then F is an automorphism of $\mathbb{C}^n$.

This conjecture is notorious for the many false proofs of it that exist in print. I myself produced two, but neither of them survived the 24-hour test, and they were therefore not published, fortunately.

Maybe some time in the future?